About the Author

Poet, activist, mother, and professor, Nikki Giovanni is a six-time NAACP Image Award winner and the first recipient of the Rosa Parks Woman of Courage Award, and holds the Langston Hughes Medal for Outstanding Poetry, among other honors. The author of twenty-seven books and a Grammy nominee for *The Nikki Giovanni Poetry Collection*, she is the University Distinguished Professor/English at Virginia Tech in Blacksburg, Virginia, and an Oprah Living Legend.

WWW.NIKKI-GIOVANNI.COM

Quilting the **Black-Eyed** Pea

ALSO BY NIKKI GIOVANNI

Poetry

Black Feeling Black Talk/Black Judgement
Re: Creation
My House
The Women and the Men
Cotton Candy on a Rainy Day
Those Who Ride the Night Winds
The Selected Poems of Nikki Giovanni
Love Poems
Blues: For All the Changes
Acolytes
The Collected Poetry of Nikki Giovanni
Bicycles

Prose

*Gemini: An Extended Autobiographical Statement on
    My First Twenty-Five Years of Being a Black Poet*
A Dialogue: James Baldwin and Nikki Giovanni
*A Poetic Equation: Conversations Between Nikki Giovanni
    and Margaret Walker*
Sacred Cows ... and Other Edibles
Racism 101

Edited by Nikki Giovanni

Night Comes Softly: An Anthology of Black Female Voices
Appalachian Elders: A Warm Hearth Sampler
*Grand Mothers: Poems, Reminiscences, and Short Stories
    About the Keepers of Our Traditions*
*Shimmy Shimmy Shimmy Like My Sister Kate: Looking at the
    Harlem Renaissance Through Poems*

For Children

Spin a Soft Black Song
Vacation Time: Poems for Children
Knoxville, Tennesse
The Genie in the Jar
The Sun Is So Quiet
Ego-Tripping and Other Poems for Young People
The Grasshopper's Song: An Aesop's Fable Revisited
Rosa
Abraham Lincoln and Frederick Douglass: An American Friendship
Hip Hop Speaks to Children

HARPER PERENNIAL

NEW YORK • LONDON • TORONTO • SYDNEY • NEW DELHI • AUCKLAND

NIKKI GIOVANNI

Quilting the Black-Eyed Pea

poems and not quite poems

HARPER ● PERENNIAL

The following poems have been printed elsewhere:

"What We Miss" was published in *Essence*, May 2000.

"BLK History Month" appeared on www.BET.com, February 5, 2001.

"No Complaints" was published in *The Black Collegian*, February 12, 2001.

"Word Olympics" appears on a bookmark for The Children's Book Council, Inc., 2000.

"Swinging on a Rainbow" appeared in *64* magazine, July 2000.

"Bring On The Bombs: A Historical Interview" appeared in *Best Black Women's Erotica* © 2001, edited by Blanche Richardson, published by Cleis Press.

"Symphony of the Sphinx" was performed by the Detroit Symphony Orchestra, February 2002.

"Meatloaf" appeared in *From My People: 400 Years of African-American Folklore* © 2002, edited by Daryl Cumber Dance, published by W. W. Norton & Company.

"Here's to Gwen" appeared in *64* magazine, 2001. "Here's to Gwen" contains the poem "We Real Cool" by Gwendolyn Brooks, 1966.

"the train to Knoxville" appeared in *The Women's Review of Books*, July 1999.

"Aunt Daughter and That Glorious Song" appeared in *Lift Every Voice and Sing: A Celebration of the Negro National Anthem* © 2000 by Julian Bond and Kathryn Wilson, published by Random House.

"The Song of the Feet" appeared in *O* magazine, November 2002.

A hardcover edition of this book was published in 2002 by William Morrow, an imprint of HarperCollins Publishers.

FIRST HARPER PERENNIAL EDITION PUBLISHED 2011.

Designed by Shubhani Sarkar

The Library of Congress has catalogued the hardcover edition as follows:

Giovanni, Nikki.
  Quilting the black-eyed pea : poems and not quite poems /
  Nikki Giovanni.—1st ed.
  p. cm.
  ISBN 0-06-009952-6
  1. African American women—poetry.   I. Title.
PS3557.155 Q46   2002
811'.54—dc21   2002066025

ISBN 978-0-06-009953-4 (pbk.)

11 12 13 14 15 RRD 10 9 8 7 6 5 4 3 2 1

The Black-Eyed Pea is dedicated to:

Contents

Quilting the **Black-Eyed** Pea

Quilting the Black-Eyed Pea

(We're Going to Mars)

We're going to Mars for the same reason Marco Polo rocketed
     to China
    for the same reason Columbus trimmed
     his sails on a dream of spices
    for the very same reason Shakelton
     was enchanted with penguins
    for the reason we fall in love
It's the only adventure

We're going to Mars because Peary couldn't go to the North
     Pole without Matthew Henson
    because Chicago couldn't be a city
     without Jean Baptiste Du Sable
    because George Washington Carver and
     his peanut were the right partners for
     Booker T.
It's a life seeking thing

We're going to Mars because whatever is wrong with us will not
     get right with us so we journey forth
     carrying the same baggage
     but every now and then leaving
     one little bitty thing behind:
     maybe drop torturing Hunchbacks here;
     maybe drop lynching Billy Budd there;
     maybe not whipping Uncle Tom to death;
     maybe resisting global war.
One day looking for prejudice to slip.......one day looking for
hatred to tumble by the wayside.......one day maybe the
whole community will no longer be vested in who sleeps with
whom.......maybe one day the Jewish community will be at
rest.......the Christian community will be content.......the
Muslim community will be at peace.......and all the rest of us

will get great meals at Holydays and learn new songs and sing
in harmony

We're going to Mars   because it gives us a reason to change
If Mars came here   it would be ugly
                       nations would ban together to hunt down
                           and kill Martians
                       and being the stupid undeserving life
                           forms that we are
                       we would also hunt down and kill
                           what would be termed
                       Martian Sympathizers
                       As if the *Fugitive Slave Law* wasn't
                           bad enough then
                       As if the so-called *War on Terrorism*
                           isn't pitiful Now
When do we learn and what does it take to teach us things
    cannot be:
                       What we want
                       When we want
                       As we want
                   Other people have ideas and inputs
                   And why won't they leave Rap Brown alone
The future is ours to take

We're going to Mars   because we have the hardware to do it . . .
                       we have
                       Rockets and fuel and money and stuff
                           and the only
                       Reason NASA is holding back is they
                           don't know
                       If what they send out will be what they
                           get back
So let me slow this down;

Mars is 1 year of travel to get there.......
      plus 1 year of living on Mars.......
      plus 1 year to return to Earth........
      = 3 years of Earthlings being in a tight space going to
an unknown place with an unsure welcome awaiting
them...tired muscles...unknown and unusual foods...harsh
conditions...and no known landmarks to keep them human . . .
only a hope and a prayer that they will be shadowed beneath
a benign hand and there is no historical precedent for that
except this:

The trip to Mars can only be understood through Black Americans
I say, the trip to Mars can only be understood through Black Americans

The people who were captured and enslaved immediately
recognized the men who chained and whipped them and herded
them into ships so tightly packed there was no room to turn . . .
no privacy to respect . . . no tears to fall without landing on
another . . . were not kind and gentle and concerned for the state
of their souls . . . no . . . the men with whips and chains were
understood to be killers . . . feared to be cannibals . . . known
to be sexual predators . . . The captured knew they were in
trouble...in an unknown place . . . without communicable
abilities with a violent and capricious species . . .
But they could look out and still see signs of Home
      they could still smell the sweetness in the air
      they could see the clouds floating above the land they loved
But there reached a point where the captured could not only not
   look back
      they had no idea which way "back" might be
      there was nothing in the middle of the deep blue water to
      indicate which way home might be and it was that
      moment . . . when a decision had to be made:
      Do they continue forward with a resolve to see

this thing through or do they embrace the waters
and find another world
In the belly of the ship a moan was heard . . . and someone
picked up the moan . . . and a song was raised . . . and that song
would offer comfort . . . and hope . . . and tell the story . . .

When we go to Mars.........it's the same thing....it's Middle
  Passage
When the rocket red glares the astronauts will be able to see
themselves pull away from Earth . . . as the ship goes deeper
they will see a sparkle of blue . . . and then one day not only will
they not see Earth . . . they won't know which way to look . . .
and that is why NASA needs to call Black America

They need to ask us: How did you calm your fears . . . . How
were you able to decide you were human even when everything
said you were not . . . How did you find the comfort in the face
of the improbable to make the world you came to your world . . .
How was your soul able to look back and wonder

And we will tell them what to do: To successfully go to Mars
and back you will need a song . . . take some Billie Holiday for
the sad days and some Charlie Parker for the happy ones but
always keep at least one good Spiritual for comfort . . . You
will need a slice or two of meatloaf and if you can manage it
some fried chicken in a shoebox with a nice moist lemon pound
cake . . . a bottle of beer because no one should go that far with-
out a beer and maybe a six-pack so that if there is life on Mars
you can share . . . Popcorn for the celebration when you land
while you wait on your land legs to kick in . . . and as you climb
down the ladder from your spaceship to the Martian surface . . .
look to your left . . . and there you'll see a smiling community
quilting a black-eyed pea . . . watching you descend

Possum Crossing

Backing out the driveway
the car lights cast an eerie glow
in the morning fog centering
on movement in the rain slick street

Hitting brakes I anticipate a squirrel or a cat or sometimes
a little raccoon
I once braked for a blind little mole who try though he did
could not escape the cat toying with his life
Mother-to-be possum occasionally lopes home . . . being
naturally . . . slow her condition makes her even more ginger

We need a sign POSSUM CROSSING to warn coffee-gurgling
neighbors:
we share the streets with more than trucks and vans and
railroad crossings

All birds being the living kin of dinosaurs
think themselves invincible and pay no heed
to the rolling wheels while they dine
on an unlucky rabbit

I hit brakes for the flutter of the lights hoping it's not a deer
or a skunk or a groundhog
coffee splashes over the cup which I quickly put away from me
and into the empty passenger seat
I look . . .
relieved and exasperated . . .
to discover I have just missed a big wet leaf
struggling . . . to lift itself into the wind
and live

A Robin's Nest in Snow

Outside the window of my den
Where I sit usually counting clouds
Or airplanes or chipmunks scurrying by
On a snowy day I still see
The nest through the flurries

Snowflakes are so delicate they melt
    On your tongue
Sit proudly
    on your shoulders
Tangle themselves
    in your braids

Last spring I didn't know
A bird had made a home
In my river birch
There was activity but I thought
It was the crepe myrtle
Only when the tree exhaled
Did the life reveal itself

The snow piled up neatly
Filling the crevice
Hopefully destroying the viruses and bacteria
That can attack the young still blind robins
And I a survivor of lung cancer nestle
Hope in my heart that no harm will remain
When Spring and birds return

The Wind in the Bottle

(For Gloria Haffer on her Sixtieth Birthday)

Twice she dreamed of rainbows
Not for the pots of gold
nor the elves basking in the colors
but the symmetry of the line
going up and down

Once she wished for wings
or at least red shoes
to ease on down the road

Often she worries
two arms one head one heart
can't protect the falling fruit

Something will stay on the tree
and rot
Something will fall
and be left behind

Twice she dreamed of rainbows
playing hide-and-seek
with the clouds

The colors defy the sun

Who kisses the wind
Good night

This is for the Pullman Porters who organized when people said they couldn't. And carried the *Pittsburgh Courier* and the *Chicago Defender* to the Black Americans in the South so they would know they were not alone. This is for the Pullman Porters who helped Thurgood Marshall go south and come back north to fight the fight that resulted in *Brown v. Board of Education* because even though Kansas is west and even though Topeka is the birthplace of Gwendolyn Brooks, who wrote the powerful "The Chicago *Defender* Sends a Man to Little Rock," it was the Pullman Porters who whispered to the traveling men both the Blues Men and the "Race" Men so that they both would know what was going on. This is for the Pullman Porters who smiled as if they were happy and laughed like they were tickled when some folks were around and who silently rejoiced in 1954 when the Supreme Court announced its 9–0 decision that "separate is inherently unequal." This is for the Pullman Porters who smiled and welcomed a fourteen-year-old boy onto their train in 1955. They noticed his slight limp that he tried to disguise with a doo-wop walk; they noticed his stutter and probably understood why his mother wanted him out of Chicago during the summer when school was out. Fourteen-year-old Black boys with limps and stutters are apt to try to prove themselves in dangerous ways when mothers aren't around to look after them. So this is for the Pullman Porters who looked over that fourteen-year-old while the train rolled the reverse of the Blues Highway from Chicago to St. Louis to Memphis to Mississippi. This is for the men who kept him safe; and if Emmett Till had been able to stay on a train all summer he would have maybe grown a bit of a paunch, certainly lost his hair, probably have worn bifocals and bounced his grandchildren on his knee telling them about his summer riding the rails. But he had to get off the train. And ended up in Money, Mississippi. And was horribly, brutally, inexcusably, and unacceptably murdered. This is for the Pullman Porters who, when the sheriff was trying to get the body secretly buried, got Emmett's body on the northbound train, got his body home to Chicago, where his mother said: I want the world to see what they did to my boy. And this is for all the mothers who cried. And this is for all the people who said Never Again. And this is about Rosa Parks whose feet were not so tired, it had been, after all, an ordinary day, until the bus driver gave her the opportunity to make history. This is about Mrs. Rosa Parks from Tuskegee, Alabama, who was also the field secretary of the NAACP. This is about the moment Rosa Parks shouldered her cross, put her worldly goods aside, was willing to sacrifice her life, so that that young man in Money, Mississippi, who had been so well protected by the Pullman Porters, would not have died in vain. When Mrs. Parks said "NO" a passionate movement was begun. No longer would there be a reliance on the law; there was a higher law. When Mrs. Parks brought that light of hers to expose the evil of the system, the sun came and rested on her shoulders bringing the heat and the light of truth. Others would follow Mrs. Parks. Four young men in Greensboro, North Carolina, would also say No. Great voices would be raised singing the praises of God and exhorting us "to forgive those who trespass against us." But it was the Pullman Porters who safely got Emmett to his granduncle and it was Mrs. Rosa Parks who could not stand that death. And in not being able to stand it. She sat back down.

What We Miss: A Eulogy

What we miss: The smell of Evening in Paris or some-
times Chanel No. 5; the bits of face powder left on the dressing
table; the little tubes of tasteful not quite trashy but still very hip
red lipstick; the almost empty bottles of off-pink fingernail polish

We miss the old fan oscillating and the grunt of the girdle
resisting its chore; the smell of Dixie Peach waiting while the
iron heats to do its touch-up; we miss the instructions: I have to
go to the church meeting and you have to heat up the dinner I left
it on the stove and don't stand in front of the windows and don't
hang on the telephone if you don't know the voice right away and
I'll be back as soon as I can and absolutely we will miss the click
of the heels on the sidewalk as they hurried off proud angry
determined . . . urging us on

What we miss: The excited chatter spreading the good
news of victory or the horrible news of setbacks always wonder-
ing why and questioning when hoping now or at least soon

We miss the gathering of the book club the garden club the
Delta Alpha Zeta sorority missionary society the quilting bee the
Wednesday night prayer group the voices lifted in prayer or song
or irritation calling for a better tomorrow whatever better may be
but knowing whatever better is is change from that which cannot
be tolerated today so tomorrow must be sought defined embraced
and prepared for and those voices from those women urged us on

What we understood: That women had to work at home and
at jobs then give back for reading hour at the library or Girl
Scouts or tri hi y then raise money for city kids to go to camp in
the country and country kids to see Washington, D.C., "Our
Nation's Capital," and all the other things women had to do to
stay sane and a woman they did largely without complaint always
without remorse frequently without encouragement but always
urging us on because He may not come when you call but He

always comes on time and we have to be ready for any number of calls: to lead hundreds of slaves to freedom; to report a lynching; to pilot an airplane; to guide nine children through a murderous mob; to sculpt; to write novels and plays and poems; to dance all over Paris and defeat the Nazis with the courage of the Rainbow Tribe; to sing arias and those soul-cleansing Blues; to do anything we are called to do because "nobody is better than you" and we believed that because of the conviction in those voices urging us on

What we accept: The love the challenge the hope they offered . . . the necessity to remember . . . the vision to follow in their footsteps while blazing new trails

What we miss: The sight of those Black women walking down sidewalkless streets carrying brown bags full of groceries or leftovers or winter clothes in summer and summer clothes in winter chiding us for missing Church applauding us for schoolwork or the recital acknowledging some small deed we did finding something good and uplifting to say . . . urging us on

This is a sacred poem . . . blood has been shed to consecrate it . . .
wash your hands . . . remove your shoes . . . bow your head . . .
I . . . I . . . I Have A Dream

That was a magical time . . . Hi Ho Silver Away . . . Oh Cisco/Oh
Pancho . . . Here I Come To Save The Day . . . I want the World
to see what they did to my boy . . . No No No I'm not going to
move . . . *If we are Wrong . . . then the Constitution of the United
States is Wrong* . . . Montgomery . . . Birmingham . . . Selma . . .
Four little Girls...Constant Threats . . . Constant Harassment . . .
Constant Fear . . . SCLC . . . Ralph and Martin . . . Father Knows
Best . . . Leave It To Beaver . . . ED SULLIVAN . . . How Long . . .
Not Long

But what . . . Mr. Thoreau said to Mr. Emerson . . . are you doing out?

This is a *Letter from Birmingham City Jail* . . . This is a eulogy for
Albany . . . This is a water hose for Anniston . . . This is a Thank-
You to Diane Nash . . . This is a flag for James Farmer . . . This is
a HowCanIMakeItWithoutYou to Ella Baker . . . This is for the
red clay of Georgia that yielded black men of courage . . . black
men of vision . . . black men of hopes . . . bent over cotton . . . or
sweet potatoes . . . or pool tables and baseball diamonds . . .
playing for a chance to live free and breathe easy and have
enough money to take care of the folks they love . . . This is *Why
We Can't Wait*

That swirling Mississippi wind . . . the Alabama pine . . . that
Tennessee dust defiling the clothes the women washed . . .
those hot winds . . . the lemonade couldn't cool . . . that let the
women know . . . we too must overcome . . . this is for Fannie
Lou Hamer . . . Jo Ann Robinson . . . Septima Clark . . . Daisy
Bates . . . All the women who said Baby Baby Baby I know you
didn't mean to lose your job . . . I know you didn't mean to
gamble the rent money . . . I know you didn't mean to hit me . . .

I know the Lord is going to make a way . . . I know I'm *Leaning On The Everlasting Arms*

How much pressure . . . does the Earth exert on carbon . . . to make a diamond . . . How long does the soil push against the flesh . . . molding . . . molding . . . molding the moan that becomes a cry that bursts forth crystalline . . . unbreakable . . . priceless . . . incomparable Martin . . . *I Made My Vow To The Lord That I Never Would Turn Back* . . . How much pressure do the sins of the world press against the heart of a man who becomes the voice of his people . . . He should have had a tattoo, you know . . . **Freedom Now** . . . or something like that . . . should have braided his hair . . . carried his pool cue in a mahogany case . . . wafted that wonderful laugh over a plate of skillet fried chicken . . . drop biscuits . . . dandelion greens on the side

This is a sacred poem . . . open your arms . . . turn your palms up . . . feel the Spirit of Greatness . . . and be redeemed

BLK History Month

If Black History Month is not
viable then wind does not
carry the seeds and drop them
on fertile ground
rain does not
dampen the land
and encourage the seeds
to root
sun does not
warm the earth
and kiss the seedlings
and tell them plain:
You're As Good As Anybody Else
You've Got A Place Here, Too

Shoulders Are For Emergencies Only

Talk to me, Poem . . . I'm all alone . . . Nobody understands what
I'm saying . . .

Have you been in jail, Poem . . . A lot of poems go to jail . . . like
a lot of women who get tired of no good men . . . Do no good
poems beat up on people . . . Do no good poems say I'm sorry the
next day . . .

I know poems get lost . . . because they're always being found . . .
There are Wanted posters . . . milk bottles . . . and lonesome
guitars in the night . . . looking for a poem to take home . . .

I know poems get neglected . . . just like doo-wop singing on the
back porch and the deacons opening church with Leaning on the
Everlasting Arms . . . people forget what got them over . . . what
saved them

What are your plans, Poem . . . Give it up . . . I hear you're a rap
star now . . . going for the Grammy and the gold . . . everybody
singing your praises . . . Do you ever miss your home . . .

The sign on I-81 says: Shoulders Are For Emergencies Only . . .
Ride me, Poem . . . I think I've got the blues . . .

I Always Think of Meatloaf

When Grandmother died the O'Neal sisters who were in their nineties and blind brought four eggs that their hen had just laid: "For Lou" which is what they called her. Reverend James was there explaining why he did not announce "Mrs. Watson's passing" because "you know how people are." Mommy seemed to know what he meant but I did not "know" how people are then though I have learned. As is the case with small towns like Knoxville many friends and neighbors brought food and drink: Ham, macaroni with sautéed onions and peppers and three cheeses, homemade breads, Apple cakes, and because it is still sort of country, butter, homemade preserves and of course the O'Neal sisters to whom Grandmother had always been very kind, especially as they lost their sight, newly laid eggs. I wanted Meatloaf. I always think of meatloaf when I want a comfort food.

My Grandmother did not like Meatloaf so it became an elegant presentation when she cooked it. In her day, even to my remembrance, you could go to the butcher and purchase a piece of round steak. The butcher would grind it for you on the spot and Grandmother always had a couple of pork chops ground with it. My sister makes a more elegant loaf as she caters and does things more upscale. Hers is a veal with pork with beef which is very Californian. Mommy buys her meat already ground and she, like many people, adds oatmeal or bread crumbs not to "stretch it" as some people think but to make it firmer. We all mix it with our hands. Grandmother taught us all that.

I like ground round, one and a half pounds is just about right. I add one beaten egg which I beat with my kitchen fork that I got from Mommy in a two-cup measuring cup. Grandmother and Gary, though not with the same bowl, both use egg bowls. It's not that I in any way dislike egg bowls, I have one and I think it is a very pretty bowl, but Grandmother and my sister both messed up the kitchen when they cook. One thing for this, another for that. Mommy and I tend to keep the kitchen neat washing and putting away as we go; using the same measuring cup or bowl for many different things and since meatloaf is peasant food it must be mixed with your hands. Grandmother taught us that.

The meat is cold so your hand will get cold while you mix so be sure to keep a little running water on warm to get the color back in your fingers. When the egg and beef are well mixed but not overly so, add your spices. But I should confess here: Lately I have been thinking of Margie's macaroni and cheese which she makes with onions and peppers. I cheat when I think about that and go to the freezer department of my local supermarket and purchase frozen peppers in a bag. I sauté them in olive oil while I do my egg and meat mixing. I add them to the bowl just before the spices. I still turn it by hand, however.

There is nothing in the world that can't be improved by a bit of garlic. Have a headache? Eat a garlic clove. Love life suffering? A little garlic in a quarter stick of butter two scrambled eggs that are angel wings light will bring him around. Scared of werewolves or the tax man or your neighbor next door? Eat lots of garlic until you are sweating it: Everyone will leave you alone. So while I don't load it up with garlic never using more than two or three cloves or garlic powder of which you only need a dash (but never garlic salt as you do not need more salt) I am generous with it. And fennel. Fennel is one of the wonders of the culinary world. I am generous with that, too. And then you need what I call the Italian herbs—thyme, rosemary, a pinch of savory. Mix those by hand, too. Now open one medium-size can of tomato sauce. Slowly mix that in until you have a nice warm feeling as the room-temperature sauce will help your hands come back to color. Now turn that into a loaf dish. Wash your hands and give it a once-over. It should look wonderful. Open a small can of tomato sauce and pour it over the top of your loaf. Take a medium-size yellow or white onion, you can actually use purple but the color will be lost in this dish, and slice it as thin as you can. Place the slices down the spine of the meatloaf. Arrange four to six slices of bacon across the top. Sprinkle a little more garlic powder and freshly ground pepper. Place in the middle of a 250-degree oven and go about your business for the next hour or so. The juices will bubble and the bacon will be very brown when it is done. Take out of the oven, let sit until it cools. Drop biscuits and a bit of salad add to the meal or if you're having a truly bad day, boil a couple of potatoes in their jackets, slather them in butter, load up on the pepper, pour any zinfandel and things will look up but if you just want to remember a wonderful woman you need to make spoonbread. Mix a bit of cornmeal, one beaten egg, and enough milk to make a smooth though runny mixture. A dash of salt, a smidgen of sugar, stir with a wooden spoon as you would grits until it is firm. Turn the batter into a round baking dish you have hand buttered with a good pat of butter. And while you wait for it to soufflé you can sit at the table and cry a little bit because there's nothing wrong with crying for the people and the things we have lost. When the bread is ready, though, you have to stop because spoonbread has to come out on time. My Grandmother taught me that.

If it wouldn't be for my Mother's moan I might forget about Africa
A cloud of sound swirling around out in the ocean out in the
ocean alone

If it wouldn't be for the way she reaches back to that small spot
at the bottom of her spine and massages it with both hands while
exclaiming "Whew"
If it wouldn't be for the way she scratches that mosquito bite on
her left leg with the heel of her right foot and catches my hair on
a slightly jagged fingernail
If it wasn't for the way she eases herself into a hot tub of soapy
water smelling all Ivory soap–like maybe there would be no rea-
son to look back and remember

*When we put Grandmother in the ground she was wearing a light
blue dress her hands were folded comfortably her face reposed her
face reposed I can't remember her hair I don't know why I can't
remember her hair maybe the wind carried it Home*

If it hadn't been for the soup on the stove it might not have
been Monday but there was soup and it was Monday and
Grandpapa knew Today is Wash Day and since I was there I,
too, washed And rinsed And blued And bleached And starched
And carried the wash to the line to give it over to wind and
sun And carried the wash to the line to catch the smell of spice
in the air and carried the wash to the line to wave to the
clouds swirling about in an ocean of sound from the room where
Black women hum

Those bits of ham or roast beef or the skin of baked chicken and
onions and carrots and cabbage and cloves of garlic and church
and club and cabaret and salt and okra to bind the stew

If it wouldn't be for okra maybe Africa wouldn't mean the same thing

But Saturday, Lord Saturday mornings, for totally mindless reasons whether Grandmother Mother Aunt Sister Black women all over pull out clean rags and head for or instruct toward the living room which is never lived in until someone gets married or someone gets dead and why that room needs dusting is beyond me but it is Saturday and we are compelled but it is american dust

The dust of Africa rests on the dressing table where Grandmother made up her face before church where Mother checked her face before work where I squeezed pimples before school

How could I forget Africa as long as I remember that dusting

I have to remember Africa each night as I lay me down to sleep The patchwork quilt my Great-Grandmother patched one patch two patches three patches more I learned to count by those patches I learned my numbers by those patches the ones that hit and the many thousand gone I learned my patience by those patches that clove to each other to keep me warm

Blackberries blueberries koala nuts yams

Of course I remember Africa just
As Africa remembers
Me

Cal Johnson Park in Knoxville, Tennessee

My favorite spot is no longer there. Just the memory
of a Street that has the same name but none of the same
memories. I sometimes wonder
if the people living on Mulvaney Street have any idea
of the history they are living over. I wonder
if in the middle of the night they hear cries
of "Leroy! Don't cut him. Leave that man alone. That's between
him and your Mama." Or the IceMan
Get Your Ice Here or the woman in the park
who sold Hot Fish! Good Hot Fish.
Or us running across Cal Johnson Park
to see what Grandpapa had brought
us. 400 Mulvaney Street.
Just like the house next door. And the one next door. All three
sitting on a hill that has been taken down. Across the street
from a park that remains. So let's salute
Cal Johnson Park.
Without it I would have no guide
to my Grandparents'
home.

This is the way I heard the story. My family is from Albany, Georgia, my mother's family that is. My father's family is from right outside Mobile, Alabama, and they don't figure in this. My great-grandmother, Cornelia Watson, for whom I am named had a daughter who my mother and her sisters called Aunt Daughter. Aunt Daughter, who may have been named Agnes or Elizabeth, was being courted by a young man in Jacksonville. The family was not pleased as the Watsons had worked hard to accumulate land and they were landowners and businessmen. My grandfather, John Brown Watson, named for the true great emancipator, was allowed to attend Fisk University because he was considered a bit of a dreamer. The family, in fact, called him "Book," and though he was wiry and strong like his mother he seemed to lack the killer instinct of his father's family. Aunt Daughter was quite taken by the young man from Jacksonville and she asked her younger brother, John, to intercede with the family for permission to marry. Everyone considered John Brown a levelheaded young man what with him having graduated from Fisk University and not Tuskegee or an A and M, so when he suggested his mother, Cornelia, whom we called Mama Dear, and Aunt Daughter travel to Jacksonville to meet the young man's family everyone thought that was a fine idea. John Brown agreed to chaperon the two women though his wife was not pleased.

The young man's family was pleased to welcome the "Georgia Delegation." They were, in fact, educated, cultivated people who were as picky about their son as the Watsons were their daughter. They planned a big gathering for the visitors with many friends and acquaintances of the young man and his family in attendance. The young man and his brother provided the entertainment. They sang a wonderful song about being "Wild About Harry" whoever Harry was and though it was a fun song there seemed to be a bit of . . . well . . .

undertow. The young man and his brother were talking about "Shufflin' Along" when they got to New York but my great-grandmother did not believe Negroes should shuffle and she didn't care at all for her baby going up to Harlem with all that wild nightlife. Mama Dear put her back up but Aunt Daughter was evidently so taken and John Brown seemed to be so approving that she let it slide.

When the company left, the family sat down to late supper. The young man's mother said: "James, why don't you lead us in thanksgiving for this company and this meal?" And James bowed his head and having noted the disapproval of Mama Dear earlier said: "Lift every voice and sing, till Earth and Heaven ring. Ring with the harmonies of liberty. Let our rejoicing rise high as the listening skies. Let it resound loud as the roaring sea. Amen." Mama Dear noted that that was a very fine prayer but she couldn't help but say this is not what she had in mind for her baby and she, not wanting to waste the Johnsons' time, hopes everyone understands why she cannot approve of this marriage. James was crushed. And so was Aunt Daughter who went on to marry a preacher and live in Baltimore. James was so dejected he declared: "I don't want to be colored anymore." But his brother Rosamond convinced him to travel to New York where they would, in fact, do very well. Everyone remembered that lovely prayer and the family would periodically ask James to say it. Rosamond thought it would be a mighty pretty song. But it wasn't until James became a big fan of the Negro Baseball League that he could allow himself to once again embrace that difficult time of his first love. He was in the stands one afternoon when "The Star-Spangled Banner" was sung and he said: "What crap. We should have our own anthem." He and Rosamond went home and that evening took that little prayer and added: "Sing a song full of the faith that the dark past has taught us. Sing a song full of the hope that the present has brought us." And when they got to that line Rosamond knew his brother was coming out of his blues for Aunt Daughter and would find true love again. Rosamond suggested: "Facing the rising sun of a new day begun. Let us march on till victory is won. PLAY BALL."

And that's the story I was told.

Blackberry Cobbler

Always with three braids . . . mostly in red denim bib overalls . . .
usually a striped tee shirt that can't decide if it is in or out . . .
my socks flopping off my ankles . . . Grandmother would tie
her starched plaid apron . . . clear the kitchen table . . . put the
butcher block board in the center . . . and sprinkle flour . . . The
chilled dough would be rolled out . . . sprinkled with ice water
to keep it workable . . . touched up in the corners . . . And then
my job . . . the blackberries from the colander that were draining
in the sink . . . that somehow found their way . . . on my finger-
tips . . . into my hair . . . against my lips . . . onto my tongue before
they made their way . . . to the table

The Son of the Sun: Raymond Myles

If one day the Sun decided not to set but to fall, wouldn't it break? Wouldn't it splinter into billions and millions of pieces? And all that glitter would wash into the earth. Some pieces would go way into the ground. And it probably would be billions and millions of years before anyone found them. Being human and unable to know what had been discovered we would probably just call it "Gold" and trade it for lesser things. But it would be the only piece of the Sun that we could hold in our hands to comfort and intrigue us.

But what would happen if, for example, someone had planted a carrot or a lovely sweet yellow squash or a wonderfully golden yam and when that fruit of the earth blossomed some youngster from New Orleans being made by his mother to "eat his vegetables" also swallowed a piece of the Sun and when he opened his mouth notes sparkled from him. You can imagine the delight. This little five-year-old boy singing like an angel from the Sun.

This young man was so comfortable in his voice; so at home with the Delight, the Love, the Faith and Commitment; so mischievously playful with this voice. As if it was a friend and not his own. Other cities might have missed Raymond but New Orleans has a history with extraordinary musicians. New Orleans knew this son of the Sun being well acquainted with genius beginning with the drummers in Congo Square to the trumpet of Louis Armstrong to the Neville Brothers and the Marsalis family. New Orleans knows her sons. What a shame that the Sun took back that which it gave. Raymond had to go to his Heavenly home before the rest of us got to know him.

Raymond released his energy to the New Orleans sky at the street corner of Elysian Fields Avenue and Chartres Street.

Holy Ground. There should be a plaque there so that other children of the sun can come to know an angel left us at this spot . . . There should be something to memorialize the dreams Raymond Myles had for his people . . . some sort of honor guard to tell us to keep pushing . . . keep searching . . . keep looking . . . for A Taste of Heaven.

No Complaints

(For Gwendolyn Brooks, 1917–2001)

maybe there is something about the seventh of June: Gwen,
Prince and me . . . or maybe people just have to be born at some
time . . . and there are only three hundred sixty-five days or three
sixty-six every four years or so . . . meaning that some things
happen at the same time in the same rising sign . . . and the same
houses in Gemini . . . but some of us might also consider the
possibility of reincarnating revolving restructuring that spirit . . .
reshaping that spirit . . . releasing that spirit . . . tucking the use-
less inside and when the useless pushes out again we restructure
again and poetry and song and praisesong go on . . . because it is
the right thing to do

we always will cry when a great heart . . . a good soul . . . one of
the premier poets of her age restructures . . . reincarnates . . .
revolves into a resolve that we now carry in our hearts . . . as all
great women and men are alive . . . not by biology but remem-
brance . . . and that's all right . . . as the old folk say . . . because as
long as they stay on the lips . . . they nestle in our hearts and those
souls which are planted . . . continue growing . . . until generations
not knowing their touch . . . their voice . . . or even the fact
that some Chicago poets are terrible cooks . . . but always fun
to eat with . . . will tell tales of having met someone who knew
someone who once watched a basketball game . . . in which some
Chicago poet cheered for Seattle at the request of some Virginia
poet who wanted more games . . . while Mr. Blakely was amazed
that a Chicago poet was even watching a game . . . and didn't
we miss him as he slipped away watching baseball . . . and what
a way to go . . . though we then did sort of know . . . that once
gone . . . he would call the woman he loved

and so we come to no more phone calls at six a.m. to chat . . .
and no more Benihana when we are all in New York . . . and no
more gossiping and questioning and trying to make sense of a
senseless world . . . no more face-to-face . . . only the poetry which
is a great monument from this Topeka daughter to the world . . .

and yet . . . there can be no complaints in this passing . . . no
sorrow songs . . . no if onlys . . . it is all here: the work the love:
the woman: who gave and gave and gave . . . no complaints of too
long or too hard . . . no injustice of accident or misunderstanding
of disease . . . just one great woman moving to the next phase . . .
and us on the ground . . . giving Alleluias

Here's to Gwendolyn Brooks. Not only one of the premier poets of America but a woman for all seasons. Gwendolyn Brooks not only wrote great poems she lived them. From the poignancy of "A Bronzeville Mother Loiters in Mississippi. Meanwhile, a Mississippi Mother Burns Bacon," which is still the most brilliant work on the murder of Emmett Till, to "The Bean Eaters," to "The Chicago *Defender* Sends a Man to Little Rock," to "of De Witt Williams on his way to Lincoln Cemetery," which Oscar Brown, Jr., turned into a wonderful song which should have been an opera.

I had no idea when I first read *Annie Allen* and wrote one of my early book reports on Gwen that I would ever meet her or visit in her home or volunteer with her to conduct a workshop for the Blackstone Rangers or be honored to call her friend. I loved the graceful poetic movement across her lines. And I admired, without being able to put into words then, the fact that she talked about things I knew.

Tyger! tyger! burning bright . . . was lovely but
> We real cool. We
> Left school. We
>
> Lurk late. We
> Strike straight. We
>
> Sing sin. We
> Thin gin. We
>
> Jazz June. We
> Die soon.

Spoke to something this Hemingway-Kerouac-reading beatnik-in-the-making child knew to be the blues which fit somehow into the church music in church and the church music in Ray Charles and led me on a quest that has yet to be satiated.

So here's to Gwendolyn Brooks and a selection of her poems which is not a choice of flavors like Baskin-Robbins or Heinz 57 Varieties but a taste of hope and love and bitter sweetness and saltiness and one of the really great poetic minds of our century. *Selected Poems* by Gwendolyn Brooks ought to be on the spaceship when we go to Mars. They offer comfort and wisdom; laughter and tears. Here's to my Miss Brooks.

the train to Knoxville

(For my father at Knoxville College)

so what would you need? ten dollars more or less. maybe less. and uncle lee. you just needed someone to say you can go to college and there is a college for you and you have to get out of cincinnati because if you don't you will probably go to detroit or maybe chicago but not back to mobile or birmingham not back down south where ugly ass white girls look longingly at you and call you nigger so maybe you will get lucky and find the ten dollars and maybe you won't but you better hurry because there just isn't much time for a sort of short guy to get a scholarship to go to college when the sort of short guy is black

and everybody was happy that uncle lee was able to get that scholarship even though you wondered when you could do quadratic equations in your head why you had a basketball scholarship but you always knew that you had to take what they were giving since that was all you were going to get but you never fooled yourself about either the taking or the giving or the needing or the having you just sort of said to yourself I'll have to see what is being offered

and it's really hard to remember that mama bell whose name you called as you awaited the transition would be kind enough to put something in front of you that made sense for you to eat though by the time you talked about it she was one of the women in your life who unqualifiedly loved you though you were always smart enough to know that no one would unqualifiedly love you if they knew who you were

and you found the ten dollars because your friends were laughing and saying you don't want to go to college you can stay here and run the numbers and the women and make a lot of money but you had purchased that dream and you were determined to stay asleep and part of the ten dollars for the train fare to Knoxville came from the women who slept with you and who were kind to you because they knew you were a special person who could go

left or right good or bad kind or mean but there was something
in you that they liked and something in you that they recognized
needed something they offered and even though they would have
given you their hearts they decided to offer you a dollar a quarter
a dime so that you could catch that train to Knoxville

and in segregated america in 1935 you go to a campus which wel-
comes you even though the upper classmen shave your head and
laugh at the fact that you don't have any underwear on because
underwear would have cut into that ten dollars or so that you
needed to take a train ride south so you smile when you meet a
girl with very long hair and a bit of a haughty air and you ask her
out to share a cigarette which you smoke and vanilla wafers with
marshmallow fillings which she eats and you tell her in no uncer-
tain terms that you are the person for her and she will marry you
and you two will have children and you will live together 'til
death does part you and she laughs thinking you are kidding and
probably the only other person who knows you never kid has not
yet been born but when she is she will sing your praises because
some folk think they can judge you and some folk think they
know but no one understands what a step you took to board that
train and now you sit in heaven watching over all of us

and we love you for all that you are have been will ever be
because you always without a doubt without a qualification with-
out a reservation loved us

Twenty Reasons to Love Richard Williams: A Poem

This is a poem for Richard Williams

1. Because I like him
2. Because he's fun to listen to
3. Because he makes white folks crazy
4. Because he produced the two best tennis players of this generation
5. Because he isn't afraid to call a white turkey a white turkey
6. Because he draws the lightning to keep his daughters from getting burned
7. Because he cried at Indian Wells
8. Because he weaves stories and catches up people in his dreams
9. His dreams were family dreams
10. His dreams were real
11. And even when folk he did it for and the folk he did it to don't like how he has done it he did it to make them all richer and safer and better
12. And if he's lucky the people he loved and made better will not be petty and jealous but will understand what he had to do to do what he did
13. And even if they don't he did it
14. And there isn't a daughter on earth who wouldn't be proud to have him for a father
15. Because he stands in for all the fathers in the prisons of prison or the prisons of drugs or the prisons of despair or the prisons of hatred or the prisons of ignorance or the prisons of guilt or the prisons of fear and the prisons of failure
16. Because he faced himself and molded himself into the dreams his daughters dream

    And they came true

17. And Richard is a true hero who is Black and proud whose daughters are Black and proud and he makes all of us proud to be Black

18. And since that is an old-fashioned idea I'll try it this way:

19. I like him because he's brave and bodacious and most especially because

20. He makes white folks crazy (PS and the black bourgeoisie, too)

So this is a poem for the man who made the world see through his eyes how beautiful Black is after all the tears and all the setbacks; after all the promises and all the laughter; after refusing to give up; after refusing to back down; after giving our word to the Lord and each other the Great Migration rolled to a heady stop on the shores of Lake Michigan.

All was not well.

following the river; following the rails; riding in box cars; riding in wagons the Great Migration rolled to a bluesy stop in Chicago. A steely stop in Pittsburgh; an unwelcome stop in St. Louis and rockabillyed over to Memphis. The KKK followed the same trail; blood hounds following the fleeing folk who only wanted to believe that Miss Liberty's light could shine on them, too.

They would trouble the water.

carrying what their arms could hold; carrying what their hearts could not let go; carrying hope and love and a song with a very different beat; as different a beat as the color of the skin of the folk who sang it to the type of hair of the folk who bought and sold it; carrying with a pride the world had not previously known all the possibility for this republic for which we stand.

And sat. in.

it was good Mr. Brown grew dismayed watching his little girl, Linda, walk past a perfectly good school to get to a school less well endowed. He wanted her treated equally. isn't that why they came to Topeka? isn't that where Gwendolyn Brooks was born? wasn't greatness possible for his little girl, too?

Thurgood Marshall thought so.
and the Supreme Court agreed.

it was good to send the youngsters south for the summer. get them off the streets. let them know where our people have labored. let them sit in Sunday school and hear the lessons. let them get to church early and hear the Deacons start a song. watch the sisters preparing a meal. the sunshine choir start to robe up. get to know it's not all cold and pavement and people with strange accents shouting hateful words.

Emmett's mother kissed him good-bye.

no. not tired. sick and tired. asking the Lord for strength. asking the Lord to guide her feet. even if He guided them to stay still. no. not tired. not tired of her feet. tired of her people being killed. tired of 14-year-old boys being castrated. tired of not being able to stop it. no sir. I'll sit today. this evening. right now. I shall not be moved. no sir.

and Martin Luther King gave voice.

and in Greensboro four young men sat down.

and in Nashville the bus terminal was bloody.

and Aretha Franklin took that sound of those pains and hopes and confusions and love. and Aretha Franklin lifted her voice in question and complaint and why not and we're going to and voiced the needs of a generation. and Aretha Franklin came. and we had a champion. late though she frequently was; not showing up when her heart was heavy. sometimes friendly; sometimes indifferent. but that voice lifted our spirits; and we changed a nation. and Legacy gives us the Love Poems.

it is the right thing to do.

Ann's Poem
(For Ann Weinstein)

This is a poem for Ann
      so   it has to be beautiful
           it has to be strong
           it has to endure

This is a poem for Ann
      so   it must have fluidity
           it must be warm
           it has to have sunshine

This is a poem for Ann
      so   if it cries it cries alone
           if it despairs it never says
           if it is scared it whistles a happy tune

This is a poem for Ann
      so   let's be sure it is prejudice free
           let's be sure it has many colors
           let's make certain it has perfect manners

This is Ann's poem
           let's let it sing
           let's let it dance
           and please please please let it paint

This is Ann's poem
           so it is
           full of love
           full of love
           full of love

A Community of Clouds

(For my 8:00 A.M. Class)

Quiet   as the spread of red calling the day awake

Quiet   as a community of clouds casually rolling by

Quiet   as the little mouse in my cupboard trying
             not to take the bait

Like   a pillow fluffing
Like   the curtains swaying
Like   my heart held
           so confidently in your hands

Quiet   as the meadow when the hawk is overhead

Quiet   as a country road after midnight

Quiet   as my footsteps echoing in the hall

           Hurrying to my class

           Knowing no one is there

Like   a sandbox when everyone goes home
Like   the ten minutes before the movie starts
Like   last call at midnight

Quiet   as my abandonment
           that I hope
           they didn't feel

Swinging on a Rainbow

The only disadvantage of air-conditioning is that it is no longer
possible to go to the local library and listen to the birds sing.
I don't want you all to think I am an old fogey which since I am
old the only real question would be fogeyness
but I think there are things missing when you can't hear birds
sing. I also like the rustle of leaves in the fall.
And the almost total quiet except for someone
turning the newspaper page in the big reading room of the
library I grew up in.
So I guess what I am saying is that a lot of reading is done by
hearing. And listening.
And it goes without saying
by smell. Never is there a book so wonderful as the one
which recalls gingerbread smells or yeast smells or sometimes
soup in the kettle just a bit below bubbling making winter
one of the favorite times
since you get soup and cheese bread and popcorn. And I try
to let my books talk about the past, hope for the future and
always remember that human beings are just
one part of the chain.
And since we are swinging on a rainbow
it would be good . . . to hold on.

For Tony and Betty

(On their Fortieth Anniversary)

where I come from drums talk . . . smoke signals . . . and the
boogaloo sets us free . . . where I come from fires glow . . . clouds
know . . . the dance you do with me . . . is the right dance . . .
May I hold you close for forty years . . . or fifty years . . . or
maybe forever

where I come from confusion reigned . . . and kings and kings . . .
did the wrong thing . . . but where I come from . . . we played the
drums . . . and did the dance by the pale moon light . . . May I
hold you close for forty or fifty or maybe forever . . . but surely for
the best of my years

where I come from . . . we never will go back . . . the garvey dream
. . . the kenyatta promise . . . where I come from . . . my African
home . . . is in my heart . . . and in your smile . . . May I hold
you close . . . for all of my dreams . . . and all of my years . . . and
all of my hopes . . . for forty . . . fifty . . . two thousand . . . three
hundred . . . all of my loving years

Word Olympics

words on pages
relax for ages
until the word catchers visit

they then clean their rooms
and pick up old blooms
so no one will ask them "what is it?"

while playing play school
they follow the rule:
home base is the dictionary

so off they fly
with a peter pan pie
and also a tinker bell fairy

Desperate Acts

(For 9-11)

It's not easy to understand
Why angry men commit
Desperate acts

It's not easy to understand
How some dreams become
Nightmares

Those who wish
And those who need
Often feel alone

It's easy to strike back
But hard to understand

9:11:01 *(for 9:11:71)*
He Blew It

It was, after all, an ordinary day. Not a Monday when no one really feels like it but a Tuesday when folk know they really just must. An ordinary morning with people checking the stock market or last night's scores and even wondering would Boston come through for the Series which has about as much chance as Chicago not breaking everyone's heart. Again. Just a regular sort of day where the real predators stretch their arms and beat their chests just a smidgen before they take their morning meeting to make their morning fortune. Some folks boarding a plane at Logan for Los Angeles were probably annoyed that Legal's doesn't open until eleven and they will have to west into the desert sun and movie money and television rights without that famous clam chowder. "All the gold," they tell us, "in California is in a bank in the middle of Beverly Hills in somebody else's name . . . "

There are only two cities worth singing about in autumn. Sure there's *Memphis in June* and things like *Way Down Upon the Suwannee River* and *Chicago Chicago* that thundering town and *take me home, Mountain Mama* but that's a state, isn't it and all of Paris in all seasons but no one would dare sing Paris in Autumn because in Autumn there is only Rome but before Rome *Autumn in New York* . . . canyons of steel making me feel 9:11 9:11 Emergency Emergency!!!!!!!

He blew it

He wanted to be president or at least his daddy wanted him to be president and he is after all as he said his father's son so where was he and why didn't he hightail it back to the White House when the first jet took the first turning of the first stair why didn't he leave the schoolchildren and order Air Force One to Dee Cee but oh someone will say he's the president and maybe they were trying to kill him but the president is only a white boy we elect every four years and even the name changes in some sort of rotation every eight years since it was mostly the republicans who didn't want FDR elected again and again though once they got to Reagan they were sorry though the country sure as hell wasn't

He blew it

When Al Gore decided it was better to be an imitation republican than a real democrat he blew the whole thing Gore had every chance to run on a strong economy and every opportunity to tell people that this nation does not have a hereditary form of government does not pass power from one generation's genes to the next but then that may have been the problem since both of them had only their lineage to recommend them but Little Bush had something more because he had a brother in Florida who was going to see to it that Florida was Bush country and Al didn't have diddly in Tennessee or Arkansas but he should have had the people because he should have had the nerve to stand up to all the Bible lovers and remind them that Solomon was not what you would call unblemished and David was actually unkind to the husband of the woman he wanted and god still went on about using them for a righteous purpose and maybe we should leave judgments to god and go on with our elections but there was something about Al that made him want to say he is his own man as if Mondale hadn't made the same dumb decision and as for me I voted green because Nader is and has been consistent and all the democrats who were angry with the greens needed to be angry with themselves for all the bad cowardly decisions that Gore made and we can point fingers all over the place but the reality is

He blew it

So Little Bush wants to be president but he wants to say his father's men are in control which is not hard to believe because we are back to being the richest nation in the world bombing the poorest nation without even the sense and compassion to call a halt for Ramadan because some tail is wagging some dog somewhere and this is a really bad flashback to a boy we unelected and will unelect his son again And since Little Bush was scared the thing to do was _his job_ which was to go immediately to the White House put a red, white and blue bandana on his head strap on his boots and shake his fist at the air and let this nation know that scared or not we would stand and Giuliani did just that and it was right so the Mayor of New York was a man while Dee Cee boys looked for safe places to land and ultimately had to go home to Dee Cee anyway but now looked extremely cowardly so threatening bodily harm to people who everyone knows did not do it may have made himself feel better but the rest of us mourned not only our loss but the loss of compassion and sense but this is what was needed:

In times of great stress the only thing to do is turn to the people who know what to do. The president should have asked the television and radio people to please give him a few minutes. He should have stood there and said: We have been grievously hurt by the attacks on the World Trade Center and the Pentagon. I am asking Congress to award the congressional Medal of Honor to all the passengers on United Flight 93 because even though the medal is normally only given in combat these brave people who did not hesitate to give their lives may have saved thousands. I have a special request for African Americans at this time. I know I have not always appreciated your special gifts of faith and patience and song but I am now asking all African Americans wherever you are to raise a song. No matter if you are driving alone listening to me in your car or teaching a class to dissect a frog in biology lab; if you are showing students how to make Web pages or scrolling your E-mail; no matter if you are changing diapers in your home or in a hospital nursery. No matter if you are sweeping the streets or heading out of your cell for your daily one hour of exercise. Please raise a song because I believe if you raise a song the world will hear our plea and maybe we will be forgiven.

But, you know what, he didn't do that.

And for that reason alone................... he blew it.

The Self-Evident Poem

It was never theirs to begin with . . . they came and took it and now it is taken back . . . that much anyone can see . . . it's self-evident . . . no further explanation needed . . .

This poem is self-evident too . . . this poem needs no further explanation . . . this poem stands on its own as its own for its own sake . . . this poem is happy

Sometimes this poem feels lonely . . . Sometimes this poem yearns for a poem to talk with and laugh with and maybe have a glass of wine with in some nice little neighborhood corner café where everybody knows your name
And sometimes this poem just wants to take a book and go to central park and read

It's self-evident that life is about the good we do not the evil that is left behind and there is so much evil in the world sitting in so many high places telling so many lies while choking the life out of the vulnerable and the helpless and you've just got to love black folks for being able to bury the lynched and the burned for being able to bear the lash and lies for finding a song to lift our spirits and send our souls to a better place

And you've just got to feel sorry for white folks who still do not understand this is another century and we just can't keep bombing the same people over and over again because we don't want to admit the craziness is home grown

So this poem prays for peace and hopes it can find another poem to peddle for peace and they find a poem which walks for peace and they find a poem which flies for peace and maybe they will all get together and raise a song that drowns the war cries the capital punishment cries and sad cries of lost people looking for an empire that was never theirs to begin with

Have Dinner with Me

Someone said:

Oh my God! Look at the birds! Those birds didn't make it.

But the birds weren't there because the birds knew . . . Felt . . . Understood the danger and the opportunity . . . The birds were gone . . . Flying in the air . . . were the people . . . Were the people who were an hour early because the traffic was always so bad . . . Were the people who wanted to be praised for their hard work and dedication to the company . . . Were the brother and the sister at *Windows on the World* who chopped the onions . . . washed the lettuces . . . kneaded the bread dough . . . opened the oysters . . . so they could send money to El Salvador . . . Nicaragua . . . Chile . . . Colombia . . . somewhere . . . anywhere . . . where a little bit of money . . . makes a big bit of difference . . . Flying . . . because there was no floor . . . to stand on

And those who cried cried without tears . . . Those who cried were without voice . . . Those who cried howled and we wished they would shut up . . . and we complained to the Super . . . and we called Animal Control . . . but they howled because they were in pain . . . They howled because they understood the loss . . . They howled because they had to say something . . . They knew they had lost the people they loved

Who went into the apartments to look after the dogs . . .
Who went into the apartments to say to the cairn terrier the cocker spaniel the adopted greyhound who had raced his heart out and was now no longer useful but someone his someone had taken him in and given him love and now that person was gone
Who told them your friend will not be back today. Your friend did not make it out of the burning building.
Who told the dogs *It's all right to come with me . . . to take you out . . . to let me feed you.*

The person you look for will not be back.

Who stopped to tell the dogs: *You have not been a bad boy.* No one came to let you out . . . You are not a bad boy . . . you did the best you could . . . and the person you love is not returning . . . was caught up in a war . . . and is no longer with us . . . went flying because there was no floor . . . to stand upon

Who went into the apartments and cleaned the Kitty Litter and said to the cats: *Your person will not be back* . . . and you have to find a new home . . . but kittens find new homes because they are young and cute . . . Cats don't find new homes . . . because they have habits . . . and attitudes . . . and memories . . . and no one wants anything with habits . . . and attitudes . . . and memories . . . and you may survive this but you will not survive that

Who went into the dark apartment . . . to tell the old lady sitting in the rocker . . . humming to herself . . . knowing . . . the news but not . . . wanting the news
Who went in to say: *Come and have dinner with me*

This is a time of neighbors
This is a time of neighborhoods
Somebody has to
Feed the fish . . . Pet the dog . . . Call the cat
Eat with the old folks

Come . . . have dinner with me

My America

(For Hugh Downs)

Not a bad country ... neither the best nor the worst ... just a place
we call home ... and we open that door ... to the tired and the
poor ... to the huddled masses yearning ... to be free ... to those
in need ... because we need ... to be needed

Not a bad country ... but adolescently indifferent ... with time
running out ... on our innocence

Not a bad country ... but attention must be paid ... to how the
bounty came to be ours ... to all the people ... who make up the
people ... that we are

A thought here and there ... a "maybe this could have been done
differently" ... the patience that is required of those who aspire
to be ... if not the best ... then at least better

Not a bad country in fact ... most likely ... the best possible
hope ... of human beings ... to exemplify differences that:
can share prosperity ... can tolerate choices ... can respect
individuals ... can teach us all ... to love

The Girls in the Circle

The girls in the circle
Have painted their toes

They twisted their braids
With big yellow bows

They took Grandma's face powder
And powdered each nose

And sprayed *Evening in Paris*
All over their clothes

They are amazed
At how they look
They smell good too

Mother may not be amused

The girls in the circle
Now tease and giggle

They look so grown up
With that high heel wiggle

Their pearls are flapping
Their dresses flow

They are so sorry
They have no place to go

Mother refuses to drive them
Anywhere
Looking like that

Barbara Bat was annoyed. Alex and the kids always waited until the last minute to wake up. Then they ran around brushing their teeth, drinking their juice and half making their beds. She was always the last Bat in the air because she cleaned up after them. This evening she called when the sun was still red in the sky. They complained but she was on time. Barbara was tired of always being late.

Watching the Bats take off early, Jerry and Pamela Squirrel sat on their deck with a nice glass of merlot. "I see Barbara got them out on time tonight," laughed Jerry. "Alex is a good man. Look at all the fruit they saved last summer. What was that? A ton and a half? And nobody to give them credit." "Well, people don't appreciate Bats any more than they do Squirrels. Times are changing. And not for the better." They let their thoughts drift to the Turtles and the Snakes who used to live in the Meadow. Both had to move because the creek was dried up. Sitting in the top of the Oak they thought about old friends. And themselves.

Momma Possum planted a kiss on Papa's cheek, as she had done for well over thirty years. They moved into the Meadow when the road came through. Papa fell into his job one night when Bobby Badger forgot to close his door. Papa and Bobby became friends since then and sometimes patrolled together. Even after Bobby's accident Papa continued to walk in the evening to be sure everyone had closed their doors. Rubbing his knees he took a glass of tea from his wife. Winter is coming, that's for sure, he thought as he stretched and got ready to patrol his neighborhood.

All day P3, as Peter named after his famous grandfather was called, darted back and forth retrieving little packages from the spots he and his sisters had hidden them. It was mother's birthday. P3, Ronni and Casey had dinner tucked away all over the meadow. When mother came home from her canning job they would have dinner on the table and a big banner saying

"Happy Birthday, Mother" flying from the door. They had worried about the chamomile tea leaves which had to come Eagle Express from England. They had worked with EE many times but it was still a tricky business to be sure not to become the payment.

Mikey, Evelyn, Cecil and Debbie Mouse were coming to their cousins' party. It was unusual for them to be in the meadow after dark but April Rabbit was not only kin she had done a heroic deed when she distracted Mrs. Hawk from Cecil.

The party was lots of fun. Dinner was delicious. Mother loved her presents especially the chestnuts, carrots and those wonderful tea leaves. P3, Ronni and Casey washed the dishes and put everything away. The Mice scampered safely home even though Barn and Hallie Owl clearly saw them by the light of that harvest moon. Papa Possum had walked by during the singing, smiled and walked on. He did miss old Badger in these rounds. What fun they had. And being distracted by memories he didn't come back to check the door.

Which the Rabbits had left unlocked.

But since the Foxes had planned to get "drive through," it was all right.

A Very Special Christmas

When I was a little girl we lived in an apartment in Wyoming, Ohio, which is sort of a suburb of Cincinnati. Actually Cincinnati was far enough away to be similar to, though not the same as, the trip to town my grandmother and great-grandmother used to make. My parents were teaching school then and Daddy even had a second job because he had a growing family and all, and we were trying to save enough money to purchase a house. All of us were looking forward to a house because I had been promised a backyard for kickball, Mommy would have a real living room, Gary (my big sister) could have a dog and Daddy could have peace and quiet.

Gary was always the extrovert—with her friends and all—but I was the Mommy's child which being a girl worked out because I became a real good cook. Gary and her friends were always doing something and going someplace with their bikes and each other. I didn't really want to go anyway so it was no big thing to me. Plus I didn't have a bike and I was kind of scared to ask for one because I always hung around the house and I always heard them talking about bills and people were going to take things back and it didn't seem fair to be asking for something when you already knew they didn't have any money for the things we already had. When all the kids at school had been talking about having TVs and we didn't have one Daddy found out that we all felt bad so he went and got one and I figured I shouldn't ask for anything else even though there were other things I thought would be really nifty to have.

The Christmas my sister got a new bike because she had out-grown her old one, I had asked Santa for skates; mostly because I didn't realize I wouldn't be able to keep up with her bike. Her old bike was what is called a sidewalk cycle and it wasn't fast and couldn't go in the street. The new one could. It was sunny that Christmas and when I went back upstairs Mommy and Daddy could tell something was wrong. When Daddy asked how did I like my skates I told him fine and how fast I could go but when I was a little girl I was very skinny and everybody said I was "all eyes." Daddy saw that I was about to cry. He asked if Santa had maybe made a mistake by bringing me skates and bringing Gary a bike. I didn't think it was my place to criticize Santa for bringing me what I had asked for so I just told Daddy I was tired and wanted to play inside with my other toys. I went into my bedroom and started working one of my puzzles when I heard Daddy say: "Yolande, I'm not going to take this. We'll just get this child a bike." And Mommy said: "But, Gus, where can you get one today?" And Daddy said: "Carlson will open up and sell me a bike." Then he came in my room and said NIKKI, PUT YOUR COAT ON. WE'RE GOING TO GET YOU A BIKE. I didn't see that he could really get me a bike but he didn't really ask my opinion. Daddy, Mommy and I got in the car and went to East Lockland. None of the stores looked open but when Daddy pulled up to the furniture store with rows and rows of beautiful bikes a man was standing in the door. The man smiled "Come right on in," and Daddy said PICK OUT A BIKE. I knew right away which one I wanted but I thought it was only proper to give all the other bikes a fair chance. I walked up and down for what seemed like forever then came back to the blue one. It was bigger than Gary's and I just knew I could outrace her and her friends who had been so haughty. Daddy shook Carlson's hand and Mommy asked if I was happy. I was the happiest child in the whole world and nobody could tell me different. The bike was strapped to the top of the car since it was a little car and I rode in the back with the window down and my head almost out to make sure nothing happened to it. I remember Daddy told Mommy if she didn't make that fool girl (meaning me I guess) keep her head in the window they'd have a doctor bill to boot.

When we got home Gary and all her friends were waiting for us, to see if I really did get two big presents for Christmas. Daddy took the bike off the car and sat it down. It was the most beautiful bike in the world and as it turned out the only one I ever owned. It was so much bigger than me that I kept it until I had a serious accident and quit riding bikes. Daddy looked at it and looked at me for what seemed like a long time. I was afraid I had done something wrong and that now I wouldn't be allowed to keep it. NIKKI? he asked. Yes, Daddy. DO YOU KNOW HOW TO RIDE A BIKE? Yes, Daddy. THIS IS BIGGER THAN YOUR SISTER'S. Yes, Daddy. OK. LET ME SEE YOU. And he stood there while I whizzed down the street and back. He smiled, which he rarely did, and told Mommy, "Well. I'll be!" Then they went back upstairs. All the kids came around to look at my second big Christmas present and I felt very special and like a for real big girl. And Gary even said I could go riding with her.

"It was tense all over the South all the time and not just because of the *Brown* decision. It was tense well before that. Things like The Depression didn't help but, my goodness, things like freeing the slaves didn't help either." She laughed. "I guess if we could have gotten rid of the tension, put it to a vote, don't you know, a lot of folk might, just might, have said Well, Let's Go Back To Slavery and Everyone Will Be Happy." It was a throaty laugh, deep like a kitten purring. "But you know those folk who live with us, who really hate us would never be satisfied. 'Til the last one is dead or so totally humiliated. What did Mrs. Parks up in Montgomery say? Why Are You All Always Pushing Us Around? Now that's my kind of woman. It just had to stop! We were running the newspaper. That's all he had ever really wanted. He loved journalism. We pushed real hard when the New Orleans bus boycott happened. We really tried to get the word out. Funny. Everyone remembers Montgomery but most folk have forgotten New Orleans. We always thought that without New Orleans Montgomery would have been twice as hard. And, Honey, it was hard enough as it was. 'Course the main difference was King. Rosa Parks was the candle, was the light, don't you know, but King was the flame. Oh, that young man used to stop by our home to talk with L.C. We always presented him as the fine young savior that he was. Everybody talking about King was unsure and unworthy and all those terms people use when they are in the presence of greatness and don't know how to react. Hhhhpf! I never knew a man so comfortable in his skin. He knew exactly who he was and what he had to do. And was smart enough to let everybody think they were teaching him. He and I used to sit here some evenings waiting for L.C. and he would start in with questions that I knew he knew what had to happen. Martin, I would say, don't work me over. I know the drill. I've watched you. And he would just crack up. Lots of folk think he got it from Daddy King but if you ever saw Momma King work a room you'd know exactly where he got it from. We'd have a mint julep which everybody knows isn't really a drink and wait for L.C.

"We didn't travel much during those days. I'm partial to trains because I'm from a teeny tiny town and the train would go through in the morning and come back in the evening, that's the way I looked at it then. It was coming and going. I don't know where I thought the tracks ended but it was like this great big play toy rumbling through and all I could think is I want to be on it. After Momma was killed and Daddy left town, but you know, we never did see Daddy again and I always thought they were together somewhere. I would dream about them and they would be all dressed up and happy. They would be smiling at me telling me to be a good girl. I guess I always thought they were together. I would cry in my sleep sometimes but now I know what I thought is they were dead only when you're a little girl you don't know that so I just saw them together. The man who killed my mother lived in town. I used to see him when I went to the store. People would talk and nudge and whisper. I always stared at him. He drank a lot but lots of folk drink a lot, and they didn't kill my mother. She was pretty. I used to hear folk say he "forced" her. It took me the longest to understand what that meant. The people who reared me were good people. They didn't want to talk about it much so I didn't talk about it. One day my father, my adopted father, took me for a walk and told me everything. We never talked about it again. What could anyone do? Momma was dead. The white boy did it. And that was that. I must have been twelve, thirteen years old. I know now he told me because I had become what is called "a woman." They wanted me to be careful. I wasn't the one who was not "careful" but that's the way we looked at things then. What they wanted was for me to be ugly and to carry myself in an ugly way so that nobody would think of me as . . . Well, you know. So I tried all my life to be unattractive. Clean. Neat. But unattractive. Wouldn't you like a cup of coffee?"

The kitchen was not the kitchen of a woman who cooked. There were fresh cut flowers on the counter, a dishcloth with wonderful little birds on it, a rack for stacking washed dishes, an oval rag rug on the floor, a round mahogany hand-planed table with six chairs. "If this table could talk," she continued. "Oh, so many people passed through this kitchen sitting at this table discussing how we were going to change the country. Thurgood Marshall was a regular and you know, there was never a nicer fellow. No matter how bad things looked he could spin a story and have all of us laughing. Wily Blanton, too. Wily had that twang so white folks never knew they were talking to a colored man until they actually saw him. Wily was a total crack-up. But brilliant. Absolutely brilliant. Those men taught all of us how to get through tough times. Some music, some laughter . . . and well, some strategy, too. My father, my adopted father, died just before I finished high school. There was never any question of going to college anyway. L.C. used to come by the house to sell insurance. When things were going well he would take us all to the movies. But he would sit next to me. And hold my hand. I have an old friend who used to always say to me: if an older person wants a younger person, the younger person doesn't stand a chance. I never thought like that. I was thrilled back then. But maybe I didn't stand a chance. Kind of like old Uncle Ernie always putting his hands in the wrong place. Who could you tell? What kind of sense could you make of it? You just worked very very hard on never letting him get you alone. Of course, the grown-ups are so strange. Don't they notice anything? Don't they see how uncomfortable, no, distressed, you are? But they just drink and laugh and leave you out there by yourself to try to figure it out. L.C. wasn't like that so maybe that's why I trusted him. Anyway, after my father, my adopted father, died and I graduated from high school I married L.C. Seemed like those were my choices: marry L.C. or get murdered." That laugh again. "Well, maybe not exactly but women have really tough decisions to make. You know who I admire? Mrs. Parks. I guess the world admires Mrs. Parks, but the older she has gotten the more feminist she has become. She's one tough old bird. People were jealous and tried to act like she didn't know what she was doing but she damned well did. She knew ever since Emmett Till that somebody had to do something. Talk about a wake-up call. The horrible murder of Emmett Till rang a resounding bell to everybody. The *Brown* decision was in but the South was having none of it. As Roy Wilkins said It Was Because He Was A Boy. Those men murdered Till to show all the parents what they would do. But Till put some iron in our backbone. Everybody had to stand up. I'm not a mother, at least I didn't birth children, but can you imagine the pain of Till's mother to go reclaim the body and then open the casket? *Jet* and *Ebony* ran the pictures as did the *Afro-American* and the *Pittsburgh Courier*. So did we. We ran a special issue. So the tension was high and getting higher. Then came Rosa Parks and King and Montgomery.

"We really thought Little Rock was, well, different. There was talk but most people were for obeying the law. Ike wasn't much of a president no matter how you cut it and his remarks about the Supreme Court were regrettable but still nobody thought it would come to what it did. The school board reassigned the students; they went to register for Central High and we thought everything would go smoothly. There was an election going on but no one thought Faubus would have a chance. George Wallace down in Alabama had said when he lost his first election that he would never be 'out niggered' again. Well, talk about 'out niggering.' Faubus just stirred up the hate but he couldn't stir what wasn't in the pot. I have never understood the depth and breadth of white hatred. I'm glad I know it's not all of them. But something so crazy happens. All of a sudden normal-looking people start to spitting at you and tearing your clothes. Normal-looking people start to kicking children and pushing them down stairs. Normal-looking people are so incensed they are calling for blood. No one ever had to tell me what it was like that Friday on Gethsemane. Everyone was screaming for His blood except for a few of His friends. The crowd was so bad He told John to take His mother home. People were calling to release that thief Barabbas. But what did He do? What had He done? I always knew what it must have sounded like. The crazy screaming. The hatred. People haven't changed all that much, have they? The city started to go crazy. You could feel the tension. Still we thought everything would go smoothly. The police chief was supposed to take care of things. We did hear rumors that people were coming from Mississippi, Louisiana, Memphis, but we weren't expecting what we got. Mobs hanging around. The national press, thank God, started to report so we weren't alone but it was frightening. Reverend Taylor was the NAACP head but he was an elderly gentleman and he thought with the coming troubles we had better get a younger person in the leadership position. He proposed that I run, which I did and I was elected. Now, I was the one to find a way.

"We started meeting with The Children to work out how this would go. I didn't want them caught off guard if I could help it. Of course, everyone knew who I was so there were phone threats and all. Still, we weren't too worried. Well, the night before The Children were to go to Central the mob was getting frantic. You could feel it all over the city. Faubus called out the National Guard and forbade The Children from entering the school. We didn't realize until too late that Elizabeth Eckford who didn't have a phone had not been notified. That's the picture you always see of the girl with the mob screaming for her blood trying to walk away. God, that was awful. But we pulled through. Still the calls, hanging me in effigy, all the threats were really bothersome. We had our guns, we're country people so we know how to hunt, and our neighbors had their guns watching the block for us. We had this really beautiful picture window in the living room. I think a lot of houses had them, those 1950s-type GI housing. I used to love to turn off the lights and watch the stars through that window. Well, when the trouble started we pulled the curtains. But the second or third night we heard the glass break and a brick came sailing through. I was coming down the stairs when it happened but I wasn't struck. The glass was flying and L.C. came running in. I think I may have been cut a little but mostly my nerves were frayed. There were too many people in my house, there was too much hatred in my hometown, there was too little possibility of help coming. Well, just everything came together or I guess I should say fell apart. You asked me what was the most thrilling part of my participation in history? I can tell you it wasn't just The Children integrating Central and being safe. Ernest's graduation was mighty satisfying. No, it wasn't the awards we all received. If a low spot was losing the paper, a high spot was reopening it even though it took ten years to do it. It wasn't even the President's Medal which never in my wildest dreams had I thought I would receive. No.

"I started crying and it just escalated on me. I went, I guess, from tears to sobs to some kind of hysteria. I just couldn't control myself. L.C. put his arm around me and started for the back of the house. That bathroom there, in fact. Reverend Taylor was at the table with some people and Chris said to him: Daisy And I Need To Be Alone. I learned later Reverend Taylor just pulled his chair up to the bathroom door with his rifle across his lap. Chris pulled me into the bathroom and looked around for the candle. We kept candles in each room because of the storms. I always like good-smelling candles in the bathroom, so he lit it and the scent of lavender flowed. Chris put the stopper in the tub and ran a hot bath. He started unbuttoning my blouse and he was talking real soft, like you do to a crying baby or wounded animal. He was kissing and whispering to me while he took my bra off. I had chill bumps but I knew I wasn't cold. He was brushing my hair back while unzipping my skirt. He kept rubbing my back and my skirt fell on the floor. He pulled my half-slip over my head taking my arms way up high. His mouth was all over me, his fingers were playing inside my ears, then his nails were softly grating down my back. I tried to push his arm and found my fingers in his mouth so I traced his teeth then his lips then his chin. He pushed my panties aside and took control. I don't know if I screamed or dreamed that I did but it seemed as if he lifted me by my middle and put me in the tub. He pulled my panties off as he settled me in the tub. We had the old-fashioned claw-footed tub so I was mostly sitting while he took the Sweetheart soap and rubbed under my arms, over my breasts, on my legs and then he put it right next to me. I got to tell you my teeth were rattling. Chris was my husband and I liked him and didn't mind doing my wifely duty but this was something else again. He practically made me sit on that soap and I broke out in a sweat. I never thought it would have been possible to want anyone as much as I wanted him right then. I was trying to pull him into the water but he just kept going over and at me with his mouth and the soap and the water. His shirt and tie were dripping and his pants were wet. I stood up because I couldn't take it anymore and when I stood he took both his hands and opened me and whipped my middle with his tongue. I felt like I was on a boat riding a fifty-foot wave. I tried to step out of the tub but I needed him to put his hands in my front and back to keep me steady, I was trembling so much. As he lifted me down my hands were on his zipper. I didn't want to wait to get his pants down, I needed him then. I don't know how we ended up in the chair but Chris was sitting there and I was on top of him. Lord, what we must have sounded like. When he didn't have any more to give I unbuttoned his pants and thanked him properly. We both just trembled and trembled. You know, Chris was much older than I and always very solicitous of me. But this time he owned me, possessed me, made me feel the power of his love without apology. He took my head in his hands and guided me back to him. He let me know how much it meant to him. We moved back to the floor where he took his pants off but the shirt and tie were too wet and too much trouble. He lifted my legs over his shoulders and all I could say was Yes. Chris said Daisy. I Want You To Remember This When The Mob Hollers Tomorrow. I Want You To Remember To Come Back Home To Me.

"They said I was brave; that I was cool, calm and collected. What I was was happy in the contentment of being totally needed. I used to go to that front window, which we never repaired until the troubles were over, pull back the curtain and holler: Bring On The Bombs, Crackers! Bring On The Bombs."

what does this mean . . . Countee Cullen taught you in junior
high . . . in Harlem . . . with that great history of renaissance but
only Langston remained . . . what does it mean when you know
you really don't want to deliver packages or be some sort of clerk
in a back room somewhere way downtown . . . what does it mean
when you know what nobody has told you YOU WERE BEFORE
HIM WHOM YOU CALL FATHER who didn't so much dislike
you as simply not understand why you were a witness that he
wasn't first and you had all this to deal with while thinking
maybe I'm not good-looking and maybe I'm not ordinary . . .
would this make you a James Baldwin

so when you are looking around and you realize you're angry
because it just ain't right that people who look like you people
who are small and black and lonely but bright and funny and
sweet can't find a way in this world and everytime you do some-
thing you think is pretty wonderful that man WHOM YOU
CALL FATHER is trying to grind you down to his size which
isn't so much small as afraid of what's out there and somehow you
keep trying to please the unpleasable so you kiddie preach in
church because at least everybody says amen and you think *have
I found a place* but you know you can't find a place when people
still look at what your heart desires and what your arms need
as the worse sin worser than lynching black men and women
worser than denying prescription drugs to old people worser than
withholding vaccinations from poor children worser than anything
because even bad-off niggers want to find something worser than
their pitiful lives and they are trying to use you and your talent
and your hopes and dreams to make themselves think they are
whole . . . would that make you a James Baldwin

and then it occurs to you If You Are A Deer In Headlights
MOVE and avoid being steamrolled MOVE and don't take the hit
MOVE and find another place to be . . . move downtown and meet
people who accept you and not judge you move to Europe and

fall in love move with your love to Switzerland and write your books and determine never to deny what your heart knows is true never turn your back on what your mind knows is right

never refuse to hear the cry of the anguished nor the laughter in the blues do it all because this one time you go round is the only time to do it so be a stand-up guy who stands up first for yourself then all the people who need an arm to lean on or a heart to hear a voice to raise for the righteousness of it and maybe that would make you a James Baldwin

Beamer Ball

Dear Frank:

   Last year was the most thrilling time for Hokie fans! That
11–0 season just did our hearts proud. But, Frank, I had to ask
myself: "How will 2000/2001 go?" I know what you're saying:
You're saying "Hey, our guys can take anyone anywhere!" But,
Frank—there is *Syracuse* at *their* place. I've cheered against
Syracuse since they were so disgraceful in their treatment of
Patrick Ewing. You remember that time. John Thompson had to
take his team off the court. And finally, when Syracuse faced a
forfeiture, the crowd settled down. Sure, I know that was basket-
ball but poor sportsmanship is, well, poor sportsmanship and I
don't much cotton to that. So you are saying: "Why are you writ-
ing this letter?" Well, Frank, we seem to have a hard time when
we go up to the northern Orange country. I am just a smidgen
worried because this could, well, ruin a great season. I know, you
are saying: "I have Michael Vick and I have Andre Kendricks and
Corey Bird and Lee and all the Hokies who will do their job . . ."
But, Frank, what if there is some sort of magic up there that they
employ? What if there is some sort of juju? You know, like Boston
had when teams played the Celtics? I know the Celtics are
basketball but, Frank, that little green man would sit on the bas-
ketball rim and bat the other teams' balls away! Even the com-
mentators would talk about it. Now, I know Syracuse is not Boston
but it is a lot farther north than most of us go. There may be an
Orange man or someone like that sitting on the uprights to swat
our field goals off; or swing down and blind the refs to our touch-
downs. Like that thing that happened to Tennessee last week
against Florida. Somebody brought something into that contest to
make the refs make that call. It pays, Frank, to be cautious.

So here's what I started thinking last year: We should help out.
Sure, we are all in the stands cheering but maybe it's time we
Hokie women did a bit more. Frank, *I recruited a team for you.*
Since the men have had so much trouble with Syracuse, we
women are ready. I know, I know— You are saying: "Well, that's

great but where will we find shoes that small?" Frank, we all mostly play golf so we have our own cleated shoes. A few of us also still wear high heels and those will dig in just fine. Not to worry; we are ready footwear-wise. So, some smarty, Jim or somebody, will say, "But, Frank, they will need helmets." We thought of that, too. We all ride bikes or know folk who do. We have all, all twenty-two of us, gotten our bike helmets straightened out. So now I'm sure you're thinking: "Twenty-two?" But what about Special Teams? Hokie ball is Beamer Ball and Beamer Ball is Special Teams but, Frank, we won't need it. The main special thing we will be doing is dyeing our hair blue. We are all middle age or actually in four cases old women. We are dyeing our hair blue because no one can tackle a blue-haired old lady. I, as you might have guessed, have volunteered to play quarterback. I have been practicing my "Vick flick." I have my appointment already to have my nails painted a nice soft pink just like my grandmother used to wear. I will be looking good, Frank; don't you worry about that. I wanted us all to have the same color nail polish but the other women pointed out that different colors will be more distracting and I think they are right. We will be going on the twentieth to have our manicures.

In case you are thinking there will be no one to run, that is not the case. The Volunteer Hokies, which is what we are calling ourselves, since the Lady Hokies are basketball and since we were not officially recruited, are of a lot of ages. Sure, I'm a bit past half past fifty but we have plenty of excellent women's studies people who believe in good health and, actually, a couple of exceptional English majors who can sit up all night writing an excellent paper get up in the morning grab a cup of coffee and come to class and make sense. Not many students can do that, so we are very proud of our ability to stay the course.

Here is my proposal: We can either go up to Syracuse with you or we can spring a Hokie surprise. If we spring the Hokie surprise, my team and I will gather at the airport. We will need only two Hokiebirds in waiting. If, by halftime, you decide you can use our expertise, we will board the birds and we'll be up there and on the field by the end of third quarter. Plenty of time to turn things our way. If you don't need us, we'll be at the field to cheer you all when you get back. See? A win-win if ever there was one. OK. You are asking: "Why a Hokie surprise?" Because we figure Syracuse players most likely have mothers and grandmothers, too. We don't want to give them a chance to have their women-folk suited up to face us. Whereas the boys can't tackle blue-haired women, it would be nothing for other blue-haired women to huddle up and crowd the line and we don't want that because of the money we have spent on our hair and nails. I'm sure you understand that.

So, Frank, we just want you to know you are not alone. We will be ready to do whatever it takes to stand by our men. We are ship sharp and Hokie ready!

Your Number One Fan,
Nikki Giovanni

Susan Smith

Ms. Susan Smith
Women's Correctional Facility
Union, South Carolina

Dear Ms. Smith:

My creative writing class and I have been emotionally involved with the public aspects of your case since inception. When the news broke that your sons were missing, because we are a class that tries to stay current, it was the news of the day. I must say, my first thought was that perhaps you and your husband had some involvement that was unstated at that time but my class was adamant that strangers had brought this tragedy upon you and your family. My class always feels free to correct me, which they vigorously did, castigating me for being "cynical" and, I think, "old-fashioned."

As events unfolded my view prevailed but then the most astonishing thing happened. The people who were crying for you were now railing against you; and I, well, I, Ms. Smith, was just heartbroken. Even though common sense said what happened did happen, what I saw was a young woman not making a choice but out of choices. What I saw was all the hypocrites who put teddy bears on the lake sort of washing their hands as if society has no responsibility. What I saw was the configuration of bad luck and perhaps tunnel vision. I write to share with you my regret.

If the train had left a bit late, if the bus had not been on time, if the keys hadn't gotten misplaced or that bit of coffee spilled on the blouse, everything might have been so different. You might have enrolled at Virginia Tech after high school, become an English major and gone on to earn an MFA in writing producing a really troubling but wonderful story about a young woman who had to let her children go because she saw no other way out. As life has unfolded you are, perhaps, living this tragedy. I wanted and want my students to see the real unfolding which is that the rain falls on some while the sun shines on others. Very little makes sense in this world. We simply try to play the hand we are dealt with as much grace as possible.

A student in my advanced class said to me: Since you feel so strongly about what happened, you should write and tell her. Sometimes a letter helps. Well, I am a middle-aged Black American. I am a poet and a mother. I have one dog, Wendy, and five goldfish, one of whom I fear is dead but I performed a coura-geous feat (for me) and rescued two dozen feeder guppies. Seven of my guppies have died but the others I see swimming around. It is getting cold and they will not last through winter but at least they weren't thrown into a tank in some Darwinian manner. I write because I don't want my students to think I don't listen to them. And to share the sadness all grown people feel when we see a young woman with awful options. I wish you the very best, whatever "best" may mean. I hope you can center the joy with the hurt; the water with the thirst.

Sincerely,
Nikki Giovanni

Emerson Edward Rudd

Scheduled to be executed by Texas on November 15, 2001[*]

Dear Emerson Edward Rudd:

Your friend in Rome, Italy, Bianca Cerri, wrote to ask if I might drop a note to you.

I must say I regret the circumstances of our first meeting. Not only do you have bad news, our football team was just beaten by Syracuse which is not the same league but sad nonetheless. Every year we are denied the right to play for what is called the National Championship Game though there can be no National Game without a National Playoff; sort of like no justice no peace. I'm a big sports fan though the same people cheat in sport as do in life. And the rest of us try to hold ourselves together as best we can, huh?

One of my very favorite writers is Ernest Gaines who recently wrote *A Lesson Before Dying*. It is too sad and I would not recommend it but a young man is in a very similar position as you and he has to teach everyone else how to be strong and brave. I always forget that I cry and cry when I read Gaines. He also wrote *The Autobiography of Miss Jane Pittman* and that's a tearjerker, too.

I'm delighted you like my poetry. I keep trying to learn something new so that I can share what I am learning. Maybe there isn't anything new but only new ways of working with old truths. My new book which is untitled as I write to you will not be out until next November. That is, if I get it turned in by December. I think I will but I have recently become a transplanted city girl living in the country so I have a pond that I clean the leaves from and I feed the birds and change the birdbaths every other day and that doesn't leave a lot of time to write though it does leave a lot of thinking time and it's always a good idea to think.

In my younger years before lung cancer and high blood pressure I played tennis. I get so much enjoyment watching Venus and Serena play. They are the true champions and to a great degree the true heroes when you consider what happened to Monica Seles a few years ago. I hope one day to go to the Australian Open and watch one or the other win. I've never been to Australia and would love to do the Outback and the Great Barrier Reef and all of it. I like traveling but it is a bit more nerve-wracking these days.

And I just wanted to write to thank you for finding yourself in my poetry.

I'm just sorry I am not answering you in some college where you are the wide receiver or maybe you are on Special Teams and you return punts or maybe you're the kicker and yesterday despite the wind and snow you drilled a forty-five footer to win the game. And even if you didn't you still should keep kicking.

    Sincerely,
    Nikki Giovanni

*Executed.

Art Sanctuary

I would always choose to be the person running
rather than the mob chasing
I would prefer to be the person laughed at
rather than the teenagers laughing
I always admired the men and women who sat down
for their rights
And held in disdain the men and women who spat
on them
Everyone deserves Sanctuary a place to go where you are
safe
Art offers Sanctuary to everyone willing
to open their hearts as well as their eyes

Sanctuary: For Harry Potter the Movie

The movie should have started with drums. Small drums maybe bongos then trap drums then the full complement of jazz drums. Silhouetted figures straddling drums. Male figures riding really big deep drums. Hands flying. Sweat flicking through the air. A spiral of light with a certain . . . well . . . heaviness implied. Followed by a Quiet. Then the Savannah. A community of elephants. The camera moving in on the baby trailing just slightly behind its mother. The bull elephant turns his head upward testing the air. Something is awry. The bull elephant drops behind the community. He wants to bring up the rear. He seems to know something. The bull elephant suddenly charges into the bush and we hear the 40 OD six go off. The bull elephant continues toward the bush and we hear over and above the drumming the report of gunfire. The elephants turn to gather round the fallen bull. The elephants try to keep him on his feet but the bull elephant is mortally wounded. The alpha female takes up the charge while the other females surround the baby. The alpha female is repeatedly shot. The shots are in rhythm with the drumming. The juvenile elephants take up the fight while the females try to get the baby elephant away. A barrage of gunfire . . . rhythmic . . . sweaty . . . heavy . . . insistent . . . intrudes. Dust is swirling. Then silence. A wearisome silence. The settling dust can almost be heard. Then the buzzing of flies. A dark cloud of hundreds no thousands of flies heads toward us. The camera however does not move. As the dust settles and just before the flies land we see, surrounded by the carnage, still standing . . . standing still . . . the baby elephant. The object of this search. He is looking at all the death and destruction. He is trying to decide: Should I live? Do I want to live with these memories? He sees the men coming toward him with nets and chains. He has to decide: Will I live? Do I want to live . . . like this . . . with these people who have destroyed everything I cherish? Then we see a flicker of light. A promise perhaps. Surely a sign of hope. Live and tell the story. Live and sing the song of your people.

"Live! and have your blooming in the noise of the whirlwind."
—Gwendolyn Brooks, *In the Mecca*

Harry Potter was just a boy who lived. Like all of us. On the forced marches to uninhabitable reservations. Through the smallpox-infested blankets. From the stench and starvation of middle passage. From the auction blocks where the unimaginable took place. From the ghettos of Europe and in the inner cities of America. From the enforced hopelessness that only a song . . . that only an imagined grandmother's hum . . . only a dream of a better day could assuage . . . A bright star . . . like a real fat shooting star comes from the back of the screen. We see a bungalow that is near destruction. We hear the questioning voices of people running to the scene. A giant swoops down from the sky on a motorcycle. He hits the kickstand down runs into the house and emerges with something bundled in a blanket. He jumps back on the cycle and heads into the sky. As the light from the cycle shoots out we follow it to the farthermost point where it turns into a streetlight dimming out. Two distinguished figures are peering into the sky . . . waiting . . . hoping . . . sending comforting looks to each other. Then *voilà!* The cycle comes down. A giant steps off with the bundle. The waiting man and woman discuss the wisdom of the baby being left with these people. "They are all the family Harry's got. Harry needs time, even in this sterile environment, to understand what has happened and how famous he is. He needs time to prepare himself," says the waiting man. "And you think," challenges the woman, "*these people* can provide the help?" The man looks at her gently: "They are all he has. We must try to do the right thing." In the background we hear a song coming up "boop boop a boom you went to school to learn girl what you never never knew before . . . *i* before *e* except after *c* and how 2 plus 2 are four . . ."

We now cut to a man and a woman sitting in a café. There are two glasses of wine, the man drinking a red and the woman having a not too expensive champagne. It is late afternoon. The sun is setting wide and very red. The man, a young man in about his midthirties, is saying to the woman, "You know this sky reminds me of something I can't remember." "That's silly," she says. "How can you remember nothing?" "No. Well, yes. Oh well. There was a giant once named Hagrid. Hagrid was a friend of my mother and father's. He loved me. And I, he. He saved me from evil by telling me who I am. And where I came from." The background music is from the *New World* Symphony. The man looks deep into the eyes of the woman. It is obvious he cares for her very much. "You never asked me about my scar," he says. She looks into her champagne glass then at the ring on her finger then up at him. "I know an evil thing struck you and left a mark I know that. But, no, I haven't asked, Harry, because I know when you know I love you no matter what, you will share your thoughts about it with me." "Well, it was my mother, you know. It was my mother's love that protected me from harm. It was the love my mother threw over me when the evil came that kept evil from being able to touch me. After the bloodshed and the bloodletting I know that some of my blood is in evil and some evil is in my blood. But I am neither the white man you think I am nor the Black man I hope to be. I'm just the boy who lived and in living I have to find my way." He called for the check and paid. They stood. "Want to go to Aruba? We can walk the beach and talk . . . " "Oh, Harry, it takes all day to get to Aruba . . ." "Not when you're with a magical guy . . ." And off they go talking about Hagrid and Hogwarts and Dumbledore and McGonagall and Ron and Hermione and Mountain Trolls and the Mirror of Erised and Quidditch and baby elephants and manatees and the vanishing Savannah and . . .

From Whence Cometh My Help:

THE AFRICAN-AMERICAN COMMUNITY AT HOLLINS COLLEGE
by Ethel Morgan Smith (University of Missouri Press)

It should be a movie. Starring S. Epatha Merkerson as Ethel Smith. She would be driving down I-81 right before the Hollins exit. There would be some smooth jazz, a Coltrane piece from *Giant Steps* or maybe something by Mingus, "Goodbye Pork Pie Hat"; the car would be a Saturn, light gray showing full use but good care. Ethel would snap her head toward the woodsy area, in a startled way, shrug and drive on. "Must be deer back there." Mingus on bass echoing. Ethel in class. Clearly older but also much more enthusiastic than the younger women. She is smiling while listening to a classmate. Ethel jerks her head toward the woods. She is sure she sees something. Let's let Brad Pitt play Richard Dillard. Ethel and Dillard are talking. She says, "There must be a lot of deer in the woods. I see them all the time." Brad (as Richard) says, "No deer in those woods since the new building went up." "But," says Ethel, "I keep seeing something moving." "It's your poetic imagination. I had a student once who wrote about being a Pilgrim . . ." and the movie fades to a line of women. Ethel stands very still and brings the women into focus. They are carrying baskets of clothes down to the creek to wash on the rocks, to be bleached by the sun, to be dried by the wind.

Ethel is talking to an African-American man who is clearly a handyman. Since Denzel already had a commitment he could not get out of, though he tried very hard, and though Morgan Freeman wanted to step in, his horse got sick, and Freeman needed to stay in Mississippi, so we are looking at Bill Cosby in his first dramatic role since his days of *I Spy*. There had been controversy about Cosby playing the handyman because some folk thought he would take away from the Slave story that needed to be told but since the tragic death of Cosby's son there is a certain haunting in his eyes and this role should actually earn him a nomination for Best Supporting Actor. "You know," he is saying "you keep jerking toward those fields." "I keep seeing deer," says Ethel, "but everybody says there are no deer." "Daughter," says Bill, "you're seeing your ancestors. That's

Oldfields. That's where the slaves lived." "What slaves? There were no slaves at Hollins." "Oh, Daughter," Bill exclaims, "when Charles Cocke arrived to build this school he had sixteen slaves. Yes, he was good to them. Taught them to read and write. But they were still slaves. The young misses who came to learn brought their slaves, too. There was a real community. Gave them that old field over there to live in. People there who still remember."

We cut to singing in the church. We watch Beah Richards as Mrs. Bruce welcome Ethel and begin the story of the community. Whitney Houston does a special gospel song while the women turn back the pages of history. We watch Sharon Stone as Mary Bishop start to take notes and work on articles for the *Roanoke Times*. Blair Underwood appears in his first period drama as Mr. Bruce. Mr. Bruce is training his young men to be perfect in the dining hall. Mr. Bruce is practically dancing from table to table. A young man spills coffee on a student. Ethel awakes from a dream. This is the story she must tell. But she needs steady employment and mentoring. Sissy Spacek playing Virginia Fowler is recruiting Ethel Smith to Virginia Tech where she will get the supplemental help she needs to complete the project. We end with Lela Rochon and Gregory Hines as Ethel and the late Rice Dobbins. Rice is picking up a book at Volume II. "Look, Mother," he says, *"From Whence Cometh My Help.* That book by that young lady who came by last winter. Let's buy it." And Ethel smiles. In the last scene we see Ethel and Rice Dobbins holding hands walking toward a green truck. The film is nominated for Best Documentary. The whole Roanoke/New River Valley is excited. The End.

Only once have I been mad at God. I was going to say angry with but that's far too polite. I was mad. A bird had fallen out of a tree and was lying helplessly on the ground. The mother bird kept trying to feed him; the father bird was on the roof to keep predators away. I was in my living room crying. I was mad at the same God that I never questioned when I was diagnosed with lung cancer. I prayed that I would not become ugly and whiny but I never questioned that it may be my time. I never questioned this same God when my father had a stroke and was ultimately diagnosed with cancer. I just packed my bags and went home to help Mommy. I didn't even question this God when Wendy, my dog, had a brain tumor and could not survive the operation. But I was mad because of the bird. And I was in no mood to hear any reasons. The reason we have God is that Mother Nature is so indifferent to individual needs. Mother Nature will send a tornado and kill thirty/forty people; she will send an earthquake and kill thousands. No one ever prays to Mother Nature because we know she doesn't listen. But God is not only just but merciful. So I was mad. I wasn't making any deals like I'll be good if you save the bird but I was clear on how could you do this? My house-mate came home in the middle of my hysteria and started making phone calls and we were ultimately able to get the bird to a sanctuary where he could be saved. And I was glad but that's only background to a miracle I witnessed.

We have a two-car oversize garage with a normal door in the middle. One morning just a bit into Spring ago I was on my way to get the mail. I opened the door and noticed bird poop just at my step. A mourning dove sort of hopped away and I smiled at her and went "Swoosh. You're messing up my doorstep." I'm always talking to the birds and even though they talk about "bird brain" I think the birds are quite smart. She hopped out of my way but I was going up the hill. Then I noticed the blood on the back of her neck. I stepped back into the house so I would not alarm her. I called Ginney, since she always knows what to do.

She suggested we put food and water out but said she didn't think a hurt wild bird could make it. "She's not wild, she's undomesticated," I protested. But nonetheless she was injured. We found an old shoe box and I put my gloves on and was going to put her in it to offer some protection from things that bother birds. As I reached to put her into the box she flew up to the roof. I remembered the little hurt robin and we were able to pick him up because his wing was broken and he seemed very tired. At first his parents protested but then I talked to them and said to them both the same thing I had said to my mother when I went to the hospital for my operation. "You have to let go now" because there is no question you want your child to live. But you need help and we are going to get it for him. But the mourning dove was so frightened she flew up on the roof.

We left for work having put the water and birdseed out front. When we returned that evening the seed was spilled over, the water was still there but there was no bird in sight. No feathers, either, which was a good sign but we concluded the bird probably didn't make it. I must say I wasn't mad at God on this one because I felt like I had done my best and it was probably Mother Nature just doing what she does. A day or two later I went into the meadow to refill the bird feeders. The mourning doves are ground feeders. I was watching the finches when I walked right upon a dove. She didn't run or fly away. She turned her head and I could see the healing wound. I couldn't believe my eyes. She had survived and more, she had said Thanks. And that is a miracle. I didn't need a miracle to believe in God but seeing that bird really made me give thanks.

"Ginney," I said as gently though as firmly as I could. We were in Kroger's going down the produce aisle looking for, if memory serves me correctly, eggplant. "My left tit just fell off." I stood gingerly, waiting to hear the teacup sort of tinkle that I expected would be the sound of one tit falling. I waited. Ginney walked back to me. "Your tit did not fall. Look down. There is no tit there." "I'm sure it did. I reached for the okra and I stretched the back muscle too much. It's fallen off." "No," she patiently explained, "it cannot fall off. You are well. Your surgeon says you are well. Your family doctor says you are well. Your nurses say you are well. You are sewed up. Nothing can fall out." Sure, it was easy for her to be so confident. Nobody had said things to her like "Gee, the size of this tumor I'd say you'll probably be dead in six months." I had, I must confess, found that a bit dismaying. Actually insensitive. He was a fucking fool. Why would anyone say something like that to somebody? "He's an oncologist," my family doctor explained. "They don't get along well with people. I'm sure he didn't mean to frighten you." He STILL frightens me. Somehow I felt he was cheering for the disease rather than for me. Luckily my surgeon was a heartier fellow better met. I do believe in another age surgeons would have simply been gunslingers. The fastest in the Wild West. They have such a gunslinger mentality. "Well, ma'am," they swagger, "we'll just have to cut that little bugger out." You actually expect them to go "Patooey" with their little ball of Red Man. I liked that. He not only made me laugh, he made me confident that if something could be done, he could do it. Surgeons will always be heroes to me.

It was Friday, February 3. He could operate Friday, February 10. There would be a lot of testing done between then and then.

I smoked my last cigarette on Tuesday, February 7, at 9:00 A.M. in the parking lot of Jewish Hospital in Cincinnati, Ohio. I don't have any trouble remembering this because I was to go into surgery at 10:00 A.M. and I, quite frankly, was unsure of the results. If I survived the surgery, it would be my last cigarette because I would have successfully had a cancerous tumor removed from my left lung. If I did not survive the surgery, well, I still wouldn't have another cigarette.

If irony and cancer can be contained in the same sentences, it's ironic that I ended up in Cincinnati. I grew up in Cincinnati. I was born in Knoxville, Tennessee, but my father was from Cincinnati and had a job waiting for him after he graduated from Knoxville College. Mother and Father had one child already and were expecting me in early June. I don't recall if I was late or early, knowing me I was probably a little late, but I showed up on June 7, and in August Mother, Father, my sister Gary Ann and I were on a train traveling north. If they had stayed in Knoxville Father could have, perhaps, worked at TVA stoking a furnace, which he had done while attending college; he maybe could have gotten a job with, say, the post office or perhaps teaching school. The most lucrative job would most likely have been "hopping bells" (bellboy) at the Farragut Hotel. Not! Whatever could be the point of a gentleman of color attending college and obtaining a degree if the end result is Bellboy? Cincinnati still has a sign at the train station that says Gateway to the South, but it was less south rather than farther south. At any rate, we stayed.

I have lived in southwestern Virginia for the past nine years. My surgeon in Roanoke was a great guy and lots of fun. He actually did wear boots and he laughs a lot. He was saying to me how much he looked forward to the surgery because I am thin. Like most American women of middle age, I think of myself on the plump side. Not enough to actually want to do something about it, but I am a huge fan of the Delaney sisters and I think Sadie has a point about exercising. At least I've moved from not caring to thinking I should care. There used to be a show on television at about 5:30 or 6:00 in the morning. Because I used to travel about two-thirds of the year, I was always up at some ungodly hour trying to wake up enough to go to an airport and catch a plane. There was this woman who came on who did a show about exercising in bed. KICK THOSE COVERS OFF she'd cheerfully yell at you. LIFT THOSE LEGS. GET THOSE BUTTOCKS WORKING. It always made me feel so much better when I turned her on. Of course, it never occurred to me to do the exercises; that was way too much trouble but just hearing someone tell you you can exercise in bed while you in fact smoked a cigarette and had a cup of coffee was quite comforting. Of course we all pay for sloth one way or the other.

My Roanoke surgeon could schedule me for Friday. He wanted to do a tracheotomy first to make sure the tumor hadn't spread. I didn't care whether or not it had spread. I wanted it out. Then if it had spread let's go for the spread. He was, of course, being prudent but I didn't have any reason to be prudent, I wanted it out. Call me a wild and crazy kid but I wanted it out. He would do the trach on Thursday; the tumor on Friday. If that was the best I could get, well, I would go for it. I called Gloria.

Gloria is the person everyone should know when something is not going to be happy. She's good on happy, too, but she's excellent on problems. She knows everybody; she never gets rattled, and for me she always is cautious. Me, I tend to fly off the handle when I'm cornered. I am a very patient person who has solid judgment until all answers are bad, then I tend to throw the dice. I am, in other words, the kind of person who will bid a six no trump because we're already five down and "they" are five on. You may as well go out on *your* cards. Game over. One way or the other. Gloria is not only a world-class friend, premier attorney, solid human being; she is chairman of the board of Jewish Hospital. "Nik," she said, "you should come here for your second opinion."

I had decided if anyone said I was operable I would go for the operation. I was planning a second opinion only if (1) they said it was not operable or (2) they said it was not cancer. I was not determined that it would be cancer but I did not want someone to miss cancer, and maybe six months later when the prediction of the oncologist came true, someone would say, "Gee, how did we miss that?" I wanted a second, and I probably would have gone to a third, opinion if they said "no cancer." I also wanted opinions if they said "inoperable." I hated the idea of "inoperable." I wanted something to be operable, since that gave me a major chance. So when I got my wish, I was prepared to go with it. Gloria said, "You need a second opinion." Well, I thought, who would I ask a second opinion of? Usually I think that's some sort of cruel joke: Second opinions. You have to ask a second opinion of a friend of the person who gave you the first opinion. You are asking the same lab or a friend of the same lab to relook

the work. Since the diagnosis agreed with my understanding of the problem, why not just go for the operation. One of the really good things about being here in the mountains of Virginia where I live now is that we in Southwestern Virginia have a long history of dealing with lung problems. I guess all the mines and the attendant problems working underground in coal and gas have given this area a lot of experience with lung problems. I absolutely love my local hospital, Montgomery Regional. I have had two operations since moving to this area and everybody is really nice. I always feel totally confident in going in that I will come out the better. They actually remember your name, tell you how glad they are you are better. No impersonal stuff here. No indifferent personnel; no running around, sitting uselessly around, no I-don't-have-a-clue-what-I-should-be-doing-now at all. People took you to the place the person who was supposed to do something to you did it then that person took you back. I never once thought my local hospital wouldn't be absolutely wonderful.

But Gloria said, "You should come here for a second opinion." "Well, Gloria, who will have time to look over my materials and stuff?" It seemed to me that the one thing you could never quickly get is a surgeon. I could see me running around Cincinnati with my X rays saying "Will you look at my X rays and tell me what you think?" And all the great big surgeons would say, "Drop them off with my nurse; drop them off with my nurse; drop them off . . ." and me getting more and more discouraged and the one thing I definitely knew is that I could not despair because we all know that disease responds to laughter or I guess I should say Health responds to laughter and disease thrives on hopelessness. I didn't want any bad news; no sad news; no nothing but people telling me I would be all right. Maybe I didn't even have to believe it. Belief is not always a necessary condition of social conventions. Lies, known lies, have sometimes been a major factor in recovery. Didn't we learn anything from Anna and the king of Siam? I wanted a happy tune. "Nik"— Gloria never raises her voice it just becomes more definite—"I think you should come here on Monday." Who could see me that quickly? "Have you ever heard of Creighton Wright?" Well, yes I had. He had been called back to service for the Desert Shield or Storm or what we in some quarters call George Bush's Folly because of his expertise on lung and heart

things. "Sure I've heard of Wright. He's a great heart and lung guy. He did all that Desert Shield work." Why was Gloria testing my current events knowledge? I read. I keep up. What's that got to do with anything? "He will see you. On Monday. At his office." I was to send copies of my X rays and my CAT scans to him so that he could look them over during the weekend.

I grew up in what is called The Valley. I took my first bus ride all by myself to downtown Cincinnati on the no. 78 bus, which went past the Cincinnati Zoo, which is a neighbor to the

Jewish Hospital. I didn't have any special reason to know the hospital. I knew General or what was called General Hospital twenty-six years ago because I was home visiting my family for my sister's birthday when I had what I considered a bit of an upset stomach and Gary said, "You are having that baby! I can see his palm prints pushing to get out!" And I said, "No. The baby isn't due until mid-October or thereabouts. She isn't pushing or anything. I just have a bit of an upset stomach and if I take an Ex-Lax or perhaps a Fleet I'll get some relief and feel better." They rushed me to General where I subsequently produced a baby boy. But, honestly, I could have sworn it was just a bit of an upset stomach. I had no such illusions going into Jewish.

It snowed Saturday. And snowed. I stood looking out my back window at the snow. How am I going to get to Cincinnati if this keeps up? And it did. Then Sunday it stopped. But there was ice and snow on the ground. It would be a long, slow drive. It was good we had decided to drive over on Sunday anyway so that we had all day Monday to be available for consultations. We didn't even take extra clothing. I knew I had to be back in time for an operation on Thursday that if successful would lead to an operation on Friday. I was ready. There was no other choice. I could handle this thing. Of course, I had decided that the best time to cry about it all would be after it's over. I really didn't want to agitate my body so I said to myself you can cry when it's over. Right now you have to listen because people are giving you choices that one will allow you, maybe to live, and one will allow you, probably, to die and you only get to

go over this stuff once. I don't believe in prisons. I don't like them. I do believe that we, society, have enough information to know that prisons don't do any good. They don't really punish the wrongdoers; they don't comfort the victims. They do send people back into the streets who are more efficiently vicious than before they left. They do, no matter how this nation puts it, have a class and color component that corresponds in other nations with "political prisoner." In the United States we charge them with drug dealing or sexual imposition. Other nations just say "We don't like you." But I have this problem with capital punishment. Society decides to kill someone who, usually, has shot a 7-Eleven clerk or something like that because if you have shot your parents down in cold blood you can plead poor parenting and get a hung jury and in so doing this very dirty, cynical business we offer a prayer and a last meal. I can see the comfort of prayer because for those who would believe or want to believe there is a God this may offer a help but a last meal? Whatever for? Is it some sort of societal recognition that the people we put to death have never had a decent meal in their lives? How cynical of us to think all is well. We feed them and read them a nighttime story . . . "Now I lay me down to sleep." I was staying at my favorite hotel with its great kitchen and excellent wine cellar. Somehow I really didn't want any food. It seemed too much the condemned person. And I definitely didn't want to tempt the Gods.

"We're the girls from Nor/folk, Nor/folk, Nor/folk: We don't drink. We don't smoke. Nor/Folk, Nor/Folk." Which was some sort of joke when I attended my first Fisk rally. We were all in Jubilee Hall singing the praises of Fisk University. I was an early entrant and there were twenty-one of us. The early entrants were two from their sophomore year in high school and nineteen from our junior year. Maybe we were too young or maybe we were too silly or maybe we got distracted but we all were mixed in with the regular class though only one or maybe two of us graduated on time. I was not among those who did. Which is not important, since "on time" is something some countries use as an excuse for fascism and "on time" is what those who want to turn back the clock use against Black people or "on time" is some sort of crazy reason to take off in an airplane in bad weather and "on time" is a demerit when you stay home to help your sneezing child.

But the only real time that counted in Nashville, Tennessee, was the time Civil Rights was pushing. The time was now.

Fisk University is a private institution. At the time of the Civil Rights Movement it was still strong and vibrant. Fisk was the first educational institution to be awarded a Phi Beta Kappa chapter. Fisk stressed a classical education. Booker T. Washington and W.E.B. Du Bois quarreled about the kind of education the "Negro" needed, and while Washington believed in a practical knowledge and Du Bois classical, Dr. Washington sent his daughter to Fisk. What a wonderful thing had Dr. Du Bois's son lived if Du Bois could have sent his boy to Tuskegee. Maybe we would all be the better for it. Fisk University knows the power of a dream. It is the school built on a song. The eleven young men and women who went out in the late 1870s to save Fisk from bankruptcy sang their way through the South to the North over to England where Queen Victoria was so taken she awarded them a substantial monetary prize. Jubilee Hall was built with that money and the mortgage was paid and Fisk became a vibrant part of the education of Black America. Our neighbor up Jefferson Avenue, Tennessee State, had another dream.

The State students were less privileged but no less capable. Tennessee State was the land grant "colored" college. To a greater degree than at Fisk, as Afro-American men were appointed president, the head of State had to satisfy the Tennessee legislature that he was not producing or "coddling" radicals. If we spun a historical kaleidoscope we would see Charles Houston and Thurgood Marshall at Howard setting the *Brown* decision in motion. By 1954 the Supreme Court ruled in a 9–0 decision that "separate is inherently unequal." Spin now to Money, Mississippi, where Emmett Till was viciously murdered. Spin again to Montgomery, Alabama, where Rosa Parks refused to give up her seat and the very young Martin Luther King, Jr., articulated the legitimate concerns of our people. Spin now to 1960 in Greensboro, North Carolina, where four young men sat down at the Woolworth's counter. We all knew this history in our bones. We felt it flowing through our veins. Tennessee State students began the Nashville Sit-ins but they were being dismissed from school for being activists. We probably will never know how many students were denied their education simply because they refused to deny their human rights. Fisk students were always involved but someone needed to step up and Fisk students did. Diane Nash, John Lewis and others stepped up. And most tellingly Jeanne Noble, president of Delta Sigma Theta Sorority, Inc., said to the sorority, "We will provide the protesting students with bail." If any one statement assured the success of The Movement, Jeanne Noble's statement did. All the other Black Greek organizations stood with Delta and The Movement survived. And thrived. And succeeded in breaking down segregation.

There is no question that segregation is wrong. I share no doubt that affirmative action is right. But segregation did this for me: Mae Fagg was my gym teacher. She brought her friend Bill Russell to Wayne High. She brought her spirit and competitiveness to us. She tried to show us another way. The Tigerbelles were idols. When I arrived in Nashville, an early entrant to college, most likely more frightened than I wanted to admit, I definitely knew two things: Fisk had Jubilee singers and Tennessee State had the Tigerbelles. The two schools are connected by Jefferson Avenue and by a park. The park was not the wise way to walk to State. We all met around Civil Rights but also State had Carla Thomas, daughter of the famed disc jockey Rufus Thomas, and a great theatrical tradition. Fisk had Du Bois and the Jubilee Singers. We all wanted to do our best for our people; for the history we heeded. We all contributed what we had; our voices, our bodies, our commitments. The Nashville connection is a story that needs telling. The Tigerbelles were The Supremes of their day, only no one knew it. They were the divas who traveled worldwide showing everyone that Black women were wonderful. Good for Black women. We are. Really. We are.

And anytime you do your best. Whatever your best is. You are a winner. You are a writer. You are telling your story. Good for all of us. You are.

Redfish, Eels, and Heidi

I think the reason I like eel is the Cave Twins. Grandmother would catch an eel and put it in the fire and it would crackle, then she'd snatch it out and they would have supper. The eel I eat now is mostly smoked but I always think of the Twins and Grandmother when I see it on the menu.

I made a special trip to New Orleans to get redfish when I first started reading Ernest J. Gaines because Grandfather and the boy went fishing and Grandfather caught a redfish, gutted it, and threw it in the fire. I'm a big fan of blackened foods: chicken, steak, fish, because of childhood reading.

I know the reason I like goat's cheese is Heidi. I would read about Grandfather and Heidi eating their hard cheese with that bit of crusty bread and somehow I always thought there should be beer to dip it in though as I got older I realized them being Swiss and all there probably was some level of fondue.

I remember a very sad story about a couple of brothers who were starving with their mother. Father had gone forth to make his fortune and when he returned he wanted to take his sons with him though I now no longer know why Mother could not go. Mother, though, in preparing them for the journey was very sad. She sewed their ragged clothes and had a special treat for their last meal together: Tonight, she said, we are going to have warm potatoes. I have adored potatoes since, though I like mine boiled. I could eat two medium-size boiled potatoes with a quarter-stick of butter, fresh ground pepper, and a good twist of iodized sea salt every day.

And then there was Stone Soup. Everybody liked to read that story as if the old beggars got away with something but I always thought they showed the village how to share. The stone started to boil when they asked for a few potatoes, then a couple of turnips, then maybe a piece of meat if some was available and just a little bit of milk and by golly if we had some bread this would be a feast! And everyone was happy. Which when we allow our better selves to emerge is always the case.

I must say I rejected all the witch stories. I did not then and do not now understand why the witch would want to eat Hansel when the woods was full of mushrooms and wild asparagus and strawberries and greens and bark for root beer and truffles in season: why eat a boy when human beings are the last thing any healthy animal will attack?

I loved the idea of sleeping on pine needles. I've got to say one of my deep regrets is that pine oils became known as such wonderful cleaners that the scent of pine no longer brings the woods to mind but rather the bus stations and nursing homes where sickness and adversity prevail instead of the freedom of open spaces. I cried for The Little Match Girl. I hate the people who tried to make that a cute story. She was poor. Her family was poor. She froze to death because of the indifference of the people inside with a fireplace and food and drink. And that was that. This is not a musical. This is not fun.

I love children's literature because it really isn't children's literature, it is folk literature. It is stories for people to carry to each other. Cinderella is a very sad story. The older sisters cutting off their feet to fit the shoe. And Cinderella herself up in the attic talking with mice. Looking for a way out. I never thought her body found a way out, her mind did. Cinderella, like any holocaust victim, left us because life had so overwhelmed her. I cheered for Snow White. Why should she stay and be abused? Why not run off to the woods where seven dwarfs would welcome her? Didn't Bess find Porgy? Doesn't everyone need sanctuary? And shouldn't literature teach us to be heroes?

My only regret about living in a visual era is that when the pictures no longer match our faces we feel excluded. In an oral age we drew our own pictures in our own minds and everyone looked like us. I never cared for Rapunzel because I had no visual on hair that long. My neck aches even now to think about it. I never identified with the selfish dummies who caused all the problems. When I sang "Jesus loves the little children" they all were in Cal Johnson Park sitting at His feet.

I like heroes. Not that stupid, racist hunter who stumbles upon the Wolf who has eaten Little Red Riding Hood and her Grandmother. That was Little Red's fault. If she had listened to her mother and stayed on the beaten path none of that tragedy would have happened. Didn't the father in "Love and Basketball" say the same thing to his stupid, spoiled son? Didn't Blunder learn the same lesson while looking for The Wishing Gate? Reddy certainly listened to Granny Fox when she smelled trouble on the way. And all of Mother West Wind's Children listened to her, since Mother West Wind protected the creatures of the meadow. And how I wanted to do that. To have a meadow and creatures to protect and love who also loved me.

And isn't that what literature should teach us. To be our own hero. To love. To care. To cry. To laugh. To live. And try to let others live, too.

In Praise of a Teacher

The reason Miss Delaney was my favorite teacher, not just my favorite English teacher, is that she would let me read any book I wanted and would allow me to report on it. I had the pleasure of reading *The Scapegoat* as well as *We the Living* as well as *Silver Spoon* (which was about a whole bunch of rich folk who were unhappy), and *Defender of the Damned,* which was about Clarence Darrow, which led me into *Native Son* because the real case was defended by Darrow though in *Native Son* he got the chair despite the fact that Darrow never lost a client to the chair including Leopold and Loeb who killed Bobby Frank. *Native Son* led me to *Eight Men* and all the rest of Richard Wright but I preferred Langston Hughes at that time and Gwendolyn Brooks and I did reports on both of them. I always loved English because whatever human beings are, we are storytellers. It is our stories that give a light to the future. When I went to college I became a history major because history is such a wonderful story of who we think we are; English is much more a story of who we really are. It was, after all, Miss Delaney who introduced the class to *My candle burns at both ends; / It will not last the night; / But, ah, my foes, and, oh, my friends—/ It gives a lovely light.* And I thought YES. Poetry is the main line. English is the train.

Don't Think

The most important thing
I know
about teaching
is that the teacher is also learning.
Don't think
you have to know it all.

The Song of the Feet

It is appropriate that I sing
The song of the feet

The weight of the body
And what the body chooses to bear
Fall on me

I trampled the American wilderness
Forged frontier trails
Outran the mob in Tulsa
Got caught in Philadelphia

And am still unreparated

I soldiered on in Korea
Jungled through Vietman sweated out Desert Storm
Caved my way through Afghanistan
Tunneled the World Trade Center

And on the worst day of my life
Walked behind JFK
Shouldered MLK
Stood embracing Sister Betty

I wiggle my toes
In the sands of time
Trusting the touch that controls my motion
Basking in the warmth of the embrace
Day's end offers with warm salty water

It is appropriate I sing
The praise of the feet

I am a Black woman

ALSO BY **NIKKI GIOVANNI**

ACOLYTES
ISBN 978-0-06-123131-5 (hardcover)

Giovanni aims her intimate and sparing words at family and friends, the deaths of heroes, and favorite meals, candy, nature, libraries, theatre, and more.

BLUES: FOR ALL THE CHANGES
ISBN 978-0-688-15698-5 (hardcover)

From the environment to our reliance on manners, from sex and politics to love among black folk, these fifty-two poems, published in 1999, offer something for every soul and every mood.

THE COLLECTED POETRY OF NIKKI GIOVANNI: *1968–1998*
ISBN 978-0-06-072429-0 (paperback)

The complete volumes of: *Black Feeling, Black Talk/Black Judgement, My House, The Women and the Men, Cotton Candy on a Rainy Day,* and *Those Who Ride the Night Winds.*

LOVE POEMS
ISBN 978-0-688-14989-5 (hardcover)

Romantic, bold, and erotic, Giovanni's 1997 *Love Poems* expresses notions of love and intimacy in ways that are delightfully unexpected, and includes more than twenty new poems.

THE PROSAIC SOUL OF NIKKI GIOVANNI
ISBN 978-0-06-054134-7 (paperback)

Giovanni's adult prose, including: *Racism 101, Sacred Cows . . . and Other Edibles,* and *Gemini: An Extended Autobiographical Statement on My First Twenty-five Years of Being a Black Poet.*

QUILTING THE BLACK-EYED PEA: *Poems and Not Quite Poems*
ISBN 978-0-06-009953-4 (paperback)

Giovanni's 2002 revelatory gaze at the world in which we live—and her hopeful poems depicting a world she dreams we *will* call home.

BICYCLES: *Love Poems*
ISBN 978-0-06-172649-1 (paperback)

In this companion to *Love Poems,* romantic love—the physical touch, the emotional pull, the hungry heart—is distilled as never before.

"An embracing, uplifting, and sustaining voice."

—*Booklist*